ROMANTIC CRUXES

ROMANTIC CRUXES

*The English Essayists and
the Spirit of the Age*

THOMAS McFARLAND

CLARENDON PRESS · OXFORD

1987

Oxford University Press, Walton Street, Oxford OX2 6DP

Oxford New York Toronto
Delhi Bombay Calcutta Madras Karachi
Petaling Jaya Singapore Hong Kong Tokyo
Nairobi Dar es Salaam Cape Town
Melbourne Auckland
and associated companies in
Beirut Berlin Ibadan Nicosia

Oxford is a trade mark of Oxford University Press

Published in the United States
by Oxford University Press, New York

British Library Cataloguing in Publication Data
McFarland, Thomas
Romantic cruxes: the English essayists
and the spirit of the age.
1. English essays—19th century—
History and criticism   2. Romanticism
I. Title
824'.7'09 PR926
ISBN 0-19-812895-9

Library of Congress Cataloging in Publication Data
McFarland, Thomas, 1926–
Romantic cruxes.
Includes index.
1. English essays—19th century—History and
criticism. 2. Romanticism—England. 3. Lamb, Charles,
1775–1834—Criticism and interpretation. 4. Hazlitt,
William, 1778–1830—Criticism and interpretation.
5. De Quincey, Thomas, 1785–1859—Criticism and
interpretation. I. Title
PR926.M35 1987   824'.7'09145   87-7873
ISBN 0-19-812895-9

Photoset by Rowland Phototypesetting Ltd
Bury St Edmunds, Suffolk
Printed in Great Britain
at the University Printing House, Oxford
by David Stanford
Printer to the University

FOR MARCUS BOGGS

Preface

THIS book examines the English essayists, Lamb, Hazlitt, and De Quincey, as representatives of the vast upheaval in European sensibility known as Romanticism. Earlier studies of the three writers have tended to treat them as somewhat set apart from the larger engagements of their age, and by considering them under the common term 'essayists' have tended somewhat to patronize them. It is interesting that except for the loose description 'essayists', which serves more as a way of laying them aside than of binding them into a significant cultural group, the three authors are not customarily treated within the unity of a single study. And when treated individually they are, with a few exceptions, accorded non-ideational discussion. Most studies of the three figures tend towards straightforward biography, simple appreciation, or attempts to place them in the periodic table of elements in minor nineteenth-century English literature.

The present book seeks to change that state of affairs. It sees all three figures as more intense, darker, more symbolic of larger situations in human experience than received opinion would have it. Above all it sees them as more interesting. Lamb, Hazlitt, De Quincey, each was a figure deeply embattled amid the convulsive disruptions and accumulating stresses that defined Romanticism. Each must be seen against the background of the spirit of the age. Each projected his personality and experience into idiosyncratic statement that has won for its author a lasting place in the pantheon of cultural achievement. It is that statement and that achievement that this book attempts to illuminate.

T.M.

Contents

Key to Brief Titles Cited

Brief titles that appear in the notes refer either to full citations occurring shortly before or to the editions listed below.

Baudelaire Baudelaire, *Œuvres complètes*, ed. Claude Pichois, Bibliothèque de la Pléiade (Paris: Gallimard, 1975–6). 2 vols.

Blake *The Complete Poetry and Prose of William Blake*, ed. David V. Erdman, commentary by Harold Bloom, newly revised edition (Berkeley and Los Angeles: University of California Press, 1982).

Carlyle *The Works of Thomas Carlyle*, ed. H. D. Traill, centenary edition (London: Chapman & Hall, 1896–9). 30 vols.

Carlyle, *Letters* *The Collected Letters of Thomas and Jane Welsh Carlyle*, ed. Charles Richard Sanders (Durham, NC: Duke University Press, 1970–). 12 vols. to date.

Carlyle, *Reminiscences* *Reminiscences by Thomas Carlyle*, ed. James Anthony Froude (New York: Harper & Brothers, 1881).

Chambers E. K. Chambers, *Coleridge; A Biographical Study* (Oxford: The Clarendon Press, 1938).

Chateaubriand *Œuvres complètes de Chateaubriand*, augmentée d'un essai sur la vie et les ouvrages de l'auteur (Paris: P.-H. Krabbe, Libraire-Éditeur, 1851–4). 16 vols.

Coleridge, *Letters* *Collected Letters of Samuel Taylor Coleridge*, ed. Earl Leslie Griggs (Oxford: Clarendon Press, 1956–71). 6 vols.

Coleridge, *Poems* *The Complete Poetical Works of Samuel Taylor Coleridge*, ed. Ernest Hartley Coleridge (Oxford: Clarendon Press, 1912). 2 vols.

De Quincey *The Collected Writings of Thomas De Quincey*, ed. David Masson (Edinburgh: Adam and Charles Black, 1889–90). 14 vols.

De Quincey at Work *De Quincey at Work*, ed. Willard Hallam Bonner (Buffalo: Airport Publishers, 1936).

De Quincey, *Confessions* Thomas De Quincey, *Confessions of an English Opium-Eater and Other Writings*, ed. Aileen Ward, Signet Classics (New York: The New American Library. Inc., 1966).

De Quincey, *Diary* *A Diary of Thomas De Quincey, 1803*, ed. Horace A. Eaton (London: Noel Douglas, 1927).

De Quincey, *Recollections* Thomas De Quincey, *Recollections of the Lakes and the Lake Poets*, ed. David Wright, Penguin English Library (Harmondsworth, Middlesex: Penguin Books, 1970).

Goethe
Johann Wolfgang Goethe, *Gedenkausgabe der Werke, Briefe und Gespräche*, ed. Ernst Beutler (Zurich: Artemis Verlag, 1948–71). 27 vols.

Haydon
The Diary of Benjamin Robert Haydon, ed. Willard Bissell Pope (Cambridge, Mass.: Harvard University Press, 1960–3). 5 vols.

Hazlitt
The Complete Works of William Hazlitt, ed. P. P. Howe, after the edition of A. R. Waller and Arnold Glover (London: J. M. Dent and Sons, Ltd., 1930–4). 21 vols.

Hazlitt, Letters
The Letters of William Hazlitt, ed. Herschel Moreland Sikes, assisted by Willard Hallam Bonner and Gerald Lahey (New York: New York University Press, 1978).

Hegel
G. W. F. Hegel, *Werke*, ed. Eva Moldenhauer and Karl Markus Michel, Theorie-Werkausgabe (Frankfurt am Main: Suhrkamp Verlag, 1967–71). 21 vols.

Henley
W. E. Henley, 'Introduction' to Hazlitt, *English Comic Writers*, Everyman's Library (London: J. M. Dent; New York: E. P. Dutton, 1946 [1910]).

Jordan
John E. Jordan, *De Quincey to Wordsworth: A Biography of a Relationship; with the Letters of Thomas De Quincey to the Wordsworth Family* (Berkeley and Los Angeles: University of California Press, 1963).

Keats, Letters
The Letters of John Keats, 1814–21, ed. Hyder Edward Rollins (Cambridge, Mass.: Harvard University Press, 1958). 2 vols.

Keats, Poems
The Poems of John Keats, ed. Jack Stillinger (Cambridge, Mass.: Harvard University Press, 1978).

Lamb
The Works of Charles and Mary Lamb, ed. E. V. Lucas (London: Methuen & Co., 1903–4). 5 vols.

Lamb, Letters
The Letters of Charles and Mary Anne Lamb, ed. Edwin Marrs, Jr. (Ithaca, NY: Cornell University Press, 1975–). 3 vols. to date.

Lindop
Grevel Lindop, *The Opium-Eater: A Life of Thomas De Quincey* (London: J. M. Dent & Sons Ltd., 1981).

Lucas
The Letters of Charles Lamb; to which are added those of his sister Mary Lamb, ed. E. V. Lucas (London: J. M. Dent & Sons Ltd. and Methuen & Co. Ltd., 1935). 3 vols.

Marx-Engels
Karl Marx, Friedrich Engels, *Werke* (Berlin: Dietz Verlag, 1961–8). 41 vols. and a *Verzeichnis*.

Middle Years
The Letters of William and Dorothy Wordsworth; The Middle Years; Part One; 1806–1811, ed. Ernest de Selincourt, revised by Mary Moorman (Oxford: Clarendon Press, 1969).

Nerval
Gérard de Nerval, *Œuvres*, ed. Albert Béguin and Jean Richer, Bibliothèque de la Pléiade (Paris: Gallimard, 1952–56). 2 vols.

Patmore P. G. Patmore, *My Friends and Acquaintance: Being Memorials, Mind-portraits, and Personal Recollections of Deceased Celebrities of the Nineteenth Century* (London: Saunders and Otley, 1854). 3 vols.

Peacock *The Works of Thomas Love Peacock*, ed. H. F. B. Brett-Smith & C. E. Jones, Halliford edition (London: Constable, 1924–34), 10 vols.

Praz Mario Praz, *The Romantic Agony*, trans. Angus Davidson (New York: Meridian Books, 1960 [1933]).

Robinson *Henry Crabb Robinson on Books and their Writers*, ed. Edith J. Morley (New York: AMS Press, 1967). 3 vols.

Rousseau *Œuvres complètes de Jean-Jacques Rousseau*, ed. Bernard Gagnebin and Marcel Raymond, Bibliothèque de la Pléiade (Paris: Gallimard, 1959–69). 4 vols.

Schlegel *Kritische Friedrich-Schlegel Ausgabe*, ed. by Ernst Behler with the assistance of Jean-Jacques Anstett and Hans Eichner (Munich, Paderborn, Vienna: Verlag Ferdinand Schöningh, 1958–). 35 vols. when completed.

Senancour Étienne de Senancour, *Oberman, texte original de 1804 précédé du Journal intime d'Oberman*, ed. André Monglond (Paris: B. Arthaud, 1947). 3 vols.

Shelley *The Complete Works of Percy Bysshe Shelley*, ed. Roger Ingpen and Walter E. Peck (New York: Gordian Press, 1965). 10 vols.

Shelley, *Letters* *The Letters of Percy Bysshe Shelley*, ed. Frederick L. Jones (Oxford: Clarendon Press, 1964). 2 vols.

Talfourd Thomas Noon Talfourd, *Final Memorials of Charles Lamb; Consisting Chiefly of His Letters Not Before Published, With Sketches of Some of His Companions* (London: Edward Moxon, 1848). 2 vols.

Trelawny Edward John Trelawny, *Records of Shelley, Byron, and the Author*, ed. David Wright, The Penguin English Library (Harmondsworth, Middlesex: Penguin Books, 1973).

Uhland *Uhlands Werke*, ed. Ludwig Fränkel (Leipzig, Vienna: Bibliographisches Institut, 1893). 2 vols.

Wordsworth, *Poems* *The Poetical Works of William Wordsworth*, ed. Ernest de Selincourt and Helen Darbishire (Oxford: Clarendon Press, 1940–9). 5 vols.

Wordsworth, *Prose* *The Prose Works of William Wordsworth*, ed. W. J. B. Owen and Jane Worthington Smyser (Oxford: Clarendon Press, 1974). 3 vols.

I

The Spirit of the Age

THE spirit of the age was Romanticism. At least it was for the half-century or more beginning in 1789 and extending through the 1840s and beyond. That date, 1789, marked the outbreak of the French Revolution. Other possible originating moments for Romanticism can be somewhat arbitrarily isolated as 1798—the year of Wordsworth and Coleridge's *Lyrical Ballads* and of Friedrich Schlegel's *Athenäumsfragment* 116—or 1781, the year both of Schiller's *Die Räuber* and of the first six books of Rousseau's *Confessions*. The latter date would best accord with John Stuart Mill's prescription. 'The "spirit of the age"', he mused in 1831, 'is in some measure a novel expression. I do not believe that it is to be met with in any work exceeding fifty years in antiquity.'[1] One need not be bound by that limit, however, but may choose instead 1774, the date of Goethe's *Die Leiden des jungen Werthers*, 'which wonderful Performance, indeed,' said Carlyle, also in 1831, 'may in some senses be regarded as the progenitor of all that has since become popular in Literature; whereof, insofar as concerns spirit and tendency, it still offers the most instructive image.'[2] Leibniz's *Nouveaux essais* and Thomas Percy's *Reliques of Ancient English Poetry* both appeared in 1765, so that year too becomes a most persuasive contender for the originating date of Romanticism.[3] Actually, as a spiritual or cultural flood, Romanticism welled up from many sources, and the seeking for a single date will always seem to have something of the factitious about it.

But if a date need be sought, 1789 will do as well as any, and perhaps better than most. 'The French Revolution', as Shelley said to Byron, was 'the master theme of the epoch in which we live.'[4] Hazlitt, whose work of

[1] John Stuart Mill, *The Spirit of the Age*. Introductory Essay by Frederick A. von Hayek (Chicago: University of Chicago Press, 1942), 1.   [2] *Carlyle*, iii. 24.
[3] Bishop Percy's collection opened up the whole realm of ballad, folk poetry, and spontaneous and naïve outpourings of spirit, in antithesis to the poetry of genre and authorial crafting favoured by the neoclassic sensibility. For the centrality of Leibniz's *Nouveaux essais*, see, e.g., Thomas McFarland, *Originality and Imagination* (Baltimore: The Johns Hopkins Univerity Press, 1985), 110 n. 65.
[4] Shelley, *Letters*, i. 504.

1825 called *The Spirit of the Age* examined some of the significant personalities of the Romantic era, elsewhere specifically identified the new poetry of Romanticism (although he does not here call it Romanticism) as stemming from the French Revolution:

This school of poetry had its origin in the French revolution, or rather in those sentiments and opinions which produced that revolution; and which sentiments and opinions were indirectly imported into this country in translations from the German about that period. Our poetical literature had, towards the close of the last century, degenerated into the most trite, insipid, and mechanical of all things, in the hands of the followers of Pope and the old French school of poetry. It wanted something to stir it up, and it found that something in the principles and events of the French revolution. From the impulse it thus received, it rose at once from the most servile imitation and tamest common-place, to the utmost pitch of singularity and paradox. The change in the belles-lettres was as complete, and to many persons as startling, as the change in politics, with which it went hand in hand. There was a mighty ferment in the heads of statesmen and poets, kings and people. According to the prevailing notions, all was to be natural and new. Nothing that was established was to be tolerated.

Hazlitt goes on, with his customary acuteness, to delineate from his personal experience the parallelism between the political upheaval and the new literature:

... kings and queens were dethroned from their rank and station in legitimate tragedy or epic poetry, as they were decapitated elsewhere; rhyme was looked upon as a relic of the feudal system, and regular metre was abolished along with regular government. Authority and fashion, elegance and arrangement, were hooted out of countenance, as pedantry and prejudice. Every one did that which was good in his own eyes. The object was to reduce all things to an absolute level; and a singularly affected and outrageous simplicity prevailed in dress and manners, in style and sentiment. A striking effect produced where it was least expected, something new and original, no matter whether good, bad, or indifferent ... was all that was aimed at.... The licentiousness grew extreme.... The world was to be turned topsy-turvy; and poetry ... was to share its fate and begin *de novo*. It was a time of promise, a renewal of the world and of letters; and the Deucalions, who were to perform this feat of regeneration, were the present poet-laureat [Southey] and the two authors of the Lyrical Ballads. The Germans, who made heroes of robbers, and honest women of cast-off mistresses, had already exhausted the extravagant and marvellous in sentiment and situation: our native writers adopted a wonderful simplicity of style and matter. The paradox they set out with was, that all things are by nature equally fit subjects for poetry.... They founded the new school on a principle of sheer humanity, on pure nature void of art.... [T]hese sweeping reformers and dictators in the republic of letters ... were surrounded, in company with the

Muses, by a mixed rabble of idle apprentices and Botany Bay convicts, female vagrants, gipsies, meek daughters in the family of Christ, of ideot boys and mad mothers. . . . They claimed kindred only with the commonest of the people: peasants, pedlars, and village-barbers were their oracles and bosom friends.[5] Hazlitt is speaking specifically of the Lake Poets, and none too kindly at that.

What he is saying, however, is all germane to the larger outlines of Romanticism, even though it by no means exhausts the scope and variety of that kaleidoscopic entity.

Indeed, exactly what Romanticism is has been scarcely agreed upon by commentators, though it is possible to list many of its characteristics. These are often most tellingly juxtaposed against the predecessor sensibility referred to as neoclassicism. Romanticism celebrates external nature ('For what has made the sage or poet write?', asks Keats, 'But the fair paradise of Nature's light')[6], which constituted a reaction against neoclassicism's love of the city and the ideal of human, not external nature. Classicism held up as its ideal the sun of Reason, while Romanticism took refuge in the moonlit realms of Imagination. Classicism satirized the vagaries of the individual ego; Romanticism hailed Rousseauistic subjectivity and Byronic egotism. Classicism sought for the general: 'Great thoughts are always general,' wrote Dr Johnson, 'and consist in positions not limited by exceptions, and in descriptions not descending to minuteness.'[7] Romanticism on the contrary hailed the particular: 'Singular & Particular Detail is the Foundation of the Sublime', wrote Blake. 'To Generalize is to be an Idiot. To Particularize is the Alone Distinction of Merit.'[8]

Other emphases of Romanticism, besides external nature, imagination, egotism, and love of the particular, centre upon a protean variety of flights from reality: into the exotic world of medieval imagining, into the radically other world of visionary oriental setting, into the world of dreams, into drugs. Of these, the imaginative reconstruction of the middle ages took special pride of place. 'What was the Romantic School in Germany?' asked Heine in a famous question, to which he readily supplied an equally famous answer: 'It was nothing other than the reawakening of the poetry of the middle ages, as it manifested itself in the poems, paintings, and sculptures, in the art and life of those times.'[9]

[5] *Hazlitt*, v. 161–3.   [6] Keats, *Poems*, 84.
[7] Samuel Johnson, *Lives of the English Poets*, ed. George Birkbeck Hill, DCL (Oxford: Clarendon Press, 1905), i. 21.   [8] *Blake*, 641.
[9] Heinrich Heine, *Historisch-kritische Gesamtausgabe der Werke*, ed. Manfred Windfuhr, Düsseldorfer Ausgabe (Hamburg: Hoffman und Campe, 1973–), viii/1.126.

What was true for Germany was equally true for England, and for European Romanticism as such. In England, the line of medieval celebration is unbroken, though richly varied, from an early emphasis in Richard Hurd's *Letters upon Chivalry and Romance* (1762), which declared that Spenser's *Faerie Queene* had unity of design in the manner of a Gothic cathedral: 'When an architect examines a *Gothic* structure by *Grecian* rules, he finds nothing but deformity. But the *Gothic* architecture has its own rules, by which when it comes to be examined, it is seen to have its merit, as well as the Grecian.'[10] The emerging Romantic rage for the medieval, as clearly represented in Hurd, eventuated in Scott's *Ivanhoe* and *Marmion*, in Keats's *La Belle Dame sans Merci* and *Eve of St. Agnes*, and still later in Tennyson's *Lady of Shalott* and *Idylls of the King* and Morris's *Haystack in the Floods* and *Defence of Guinevere*. Indeed, it is hardly possible to overestimate, however difficult it may be to comprehend the ramifications of, the importance of medieval imagining for Romanticism.

Scarcely less important, however, is the emphasis on visionary orientalism. Coleridge, who rendered rich homage to Romantic medievalism in his *Christabel*, rendered equally rich homage to Romantic orientalism in his *Kubla Khan*. Just as the all-pervading breath of the medieval is found not only in high Romanticism, but as the conditioning climate for the popularly orientated Gothic novels, and—still more intertwined in the popular bases of nineteenth-century culture—in the architecture of clapboard houses in the American Middle West, so too does Romantic orientalism appear in dispersed and divergent forms, ranging all the way from Byron's having his portrait taken in oriental garb to Schopenhauer's using the philosophy of India as an element in his own philosophic nihilism. A standard secondary work on Emerson is called *Emerson and Asia*, and Friedrich Schlegel in 1808 produced an influential treatise called *Uber die Sprache und Weisheit der Indier*. Indeed, both Friedrich Schlegel and his brother Wilhelm actually learned Sanskrit, and Wilhelm translated the *Bhagavad-Gita* and the *Ramayana* into Latin.

The philological labours of the Schlegel brothers were here harvesting a Sanskritist tradition inaugurated in the late eighteenth century by

[10]*The Works of Richard Hurd, D.D., Lord Bishop of Worcester. In Eight Volumes* (London: Printed for T. Cadell and W. Davies, Strand, 1811), iv. 296. Hurd also says that Shakespeare 'is greater when he uses *Gothic* manners and machinery, than when he employs classical: . . . the former have, by their nature and genius, the advantage of the latter in producing the *sublime*' (p. 295).

the Briton Sir William Jones, and sustained by their German contemporaries, the scholars Franz Bopp and Jakob Grimm. Alongside the imaginations of scholars, the imaginations of poets were also inflamed by oriental visions. Victor Hugo's poems, *Les Orientales*, are no less significant of this fact than Goethe's poems called *West-östlicher Divan*, Byron's *Turkish Tales* no less significant than Moore's *Lalla Rookh, an Oriental Romance*. Chateaubriand, Nerval, and Lamartine, among others, all actually journeyed to the East and left records of their travels. In short, it may sometimes seem that 'It is in the Orient', as Friedrich Schlegel proclaimed in 1803, 'that we must seek the highest Romanticism.'[11]

The world of dreams and the world of drugs offered alternative realms of escape. Indeed, both were intertwined with one another, as well as with the geographic and temporal otherness of medievalism and orientalism. Coleridge's *Kubla Khan*, cited above as witness to Romantic orientalism, is also witness to dreams and drugs, for its subtitle is 'A Vision in a Dream', and it is prefaced by a note explaining its inception in an opium dream. De Quincey, too, intertwined Romantic dreaming, Romantic drug-taking, and Romantic orientalism in his *Confessions of an English Opium-Eater*:

Southern Asia, in general, is the seat of awful images and associations. . . . It contributes much to these feelings that Southern Asia is, and has been for thousands of years, the part of the earth most swarming with human life, the great *officina gentium*. Man is a weed in those regions. The vast empires, also, into which the enormous population of Asia has always been cast, give a further sublimity to the feelings associated with all Oriental names or images. In China, over and above what it has in common with the rest of Southern Asia, I am terrified by the modes of life, by the manners, and the barrier of utter abhorrence, and want of sympathy placed between us by feelings deeper than I can analyze. . . . All this, and much more than I can say or have time to say, the reader must enter into before he can comprehend the unimaginable horror which these dreams of Oriental imagery and mythological tortures impressed upon me.[12]

Other emphases of Romanticism were a preoccupation with melancholy, and a preoccupation with solitude. 'J'écoute, j'appelle, je n'entends pas ma voix elle-même,' exclaimed Senancour's Oberman in 1804 (Senancour's book became 'un bréviaire du romantisme' for Sainte-Beuve, for Nodier, for George Sand, for Liszt),[13] 'et je reste

[11] *Schlegel*, ii. 320.   [12] De Quincey, *Confessions*, 95.
[13] Béatrice Didier, 'Préface' to Senancour's *Oberman* (Paris: Le Livre de Poche, 1984), 14.

dans un vide intolérable, seul, perdu, incertain, pressé d'inquiétude et d'étonnement, au milieu des ombres errantes, dans l'espace impalpable et muet.'—'I listen, I call, I cannot even hear my voice, and I am left in an intolerable emptiness, alone, lost, uncertain, borne down by inquietude and astonishment, amidst errant shadows, in intangible and silent space.'[14] The Romantics exhibited a preoccupation with suicide as well.[15]Consider the implications of Nodier's title of 1806: *Les Tristes, ou mélanges tirés des tablettes d'un suicidé.* On more familiar ground, we need only cast our minds back to the suicides of Werther, of Chateaubriand's Atala, of Kleist's Penthesilea, of Vigny's Chatterton, or to the declaration in Friedrich Schlegel's *Lucinde* that 'For a human being who is a human being, there is no death other than his own self-induced death, his suicide.'[16]

Still other Romantic motifs cluster around the notion of process. The Romantic period was a world of accelerating change; governing philosophical ideas of immutable substance, as Ernst Cassirer has emphasized, had given way to protean ideas of function.[17] Everything was in flux. The spectre that the *Communist Manifesto* in 1848 proclaimed to be haunting Europe,[18] though designated as Communism, was more deeply the change from conceptions of substance to conceptions of process. As Engels said later: 'The great basic thought that the world is not to be comprehended as a complex of ready-made *things*, but as a complex of *processes*, in which the things apparently stable, no less than their mind-images in our heads, the concepts, go through an uninterrupted change of coming-into-being and passing-away . . . this

---

[14] *Senancour*, iii. 167.

[15] The theme of suicide was naturally linked to the themes of melancholy and of solitude. Alongside the plaint of Oberman, consider that of Chateaubriand's René: 'Hélas! j'étais seul, seul sur la terre! Une langueur secrète s'emparait de mon corps. Ce dégoût de la vie que j'avais ressenti dès mon enfance revenait avec une force nouvelle. Bientôt mon cœur ne fournit plus d'aliment à ma pensée, et je ne m'apercevais de mon existence que par un profond sentiment d'ennui.' (*Chateaubriand*, i. 87). Accordingly, it is only a few paragraphs later that René finds himself contemplating suicide.

[16]*Schlegel*, v. 90. Again: 'Der ist frey, der Hand an sich selbst legt, um sich selbst zu zerstören, so bald es Zeit ist, das ist die Bestimmung des Menschen!' (p. 89).

[17] e.g., 'Language, art, myth, religion are no isolated, random creations. They are held together by a common bond. But this bond is not a *vinculum substantiale*, as it was conceived and described in scholastic thought; it is rather a *vinculum functionale*,' (Ernst Cassirer, *An Essay on Man: An Introduction to a Philosophy of Human Culture* (New Haven and London: Yale University Press, 1970 [1944]), 68). See further Cassirer, *Substance and Function and Einstein's Theory of Relativity*, trans. William Curtis Swabey and Marie Collins Swabey (New York: Dover Publications, 1953 [1923]).

[18]*Marx-Engels*, iv. 461.

great fundamental thought has ... thoroughly permeated ordinary consciousness.'[19] Everything was in flux. The very nature of poetry was conceived as flux, and rigidities of form and genre were washed away in the current. Thus De Quincey in 1803: 'Poetry has been properly enough termed inspiration. ... A man of genius (whether addressing the imagination or the heart) pours forth his unpremeditated torrents of sublimity—of beauty—of pathos, he knows not—he cares not—how!'[20] How much this sentiment represents the spirit of the age may be gauged by considering that it was produced by a 17-year-old boy. Those more mature shared the sentiment as well. 'All good poetry', insisted Wordsworth, 'is the spontaneous overflow of powerful feelings.'[21] 'The poem entitled *Mont Blanc*', commented Shelley, was 'an undisciplined overflowing of the soul.'[22] 'Shelley,' observed Mary Shelley, '. . . was thrown on his own resources, and on the inspiration of his own soul; and wrote because his mind overflowed.'[23]

Everything was in flux. A new fascination with electrical dynamism permeated metaphorical conceptions: 'It is impossible to read the compositions of the most celebrated writers of the present day', said Shelley in 1821, 'without being startled with the electric life which burns within their words.'[24] The fascination with electrical current was paralleled by rapidly eroding confidence in the monolithic certainties of the past, a flowing away of old convictions: the rise of biblical Higher Criticism is metaphorically compatible in its effect with the replacement of the concept of inert matter with that of electrical lines of force. Volta, Galvani, Oersted, and Faraday in one line, Spinoza, Eichhorn, and D. F. Strauss in another, witness the gathering hegemony of process in Romantic conceiving. (The theological historian Owen Chadwick documents the gradual replacement, in the century and a half between Bossuet and Newman, of theological ideals of permanence by those of process.[25]) Both currents, indeed, underlie the fictional symbolism of Mary Shelley's *Frankenstein*.

The concept of electrical current, in its power, universality, and mystery, was a particularly potent motivator in Romantic awareness. Coleridge, speaking in 1816 of the replacement of Newton's thought,

---

[19] Ibid. xxi. 293.   [20] De Quincey, *Diary*, 169.   [21] Wordsworth, *Prose*, i. 126.
[22] *Shelley*, vi. 88.   [23] Ibid. iv. 79.   [24] Ibid. vii. 140
[25] Owen Chadwick, *From Bossuet to Newman: The Idea of Doctrinal Development* (Cambridge: Cambridge University Press, 1957).

which as 'the corpuscular system and mechanical theory' dominated the eighteenth century, says:

And now a new light was struck by the discovery of electricity, and, in every sense of the word, both playful and serious, both for good and for evil, it may be affirmed to have electrified the whole frame of natural philosophy. . . . Henceforward the new path, thus brilliantly opened, became the common road to all departments of knowledge: and, to this moment, it has been pursued with an eagerness and almost epidemic enthusiasm which, scarcely less than its political revolutions, characterise the spirit of the age.[26]

If electricity was the chief underlying symbol of the new emphasis on process, it was nevertheless only one of the metaphorical representations of current that indicated the shift from ṣtasis to process. Particularly in the world of literature and poetry, an increased import attached to rivers, torrents, cataracts, and other flowings of water. The sounding cataract haunted the Romantics like a passion; for an instance of what Keats terms 'the solid roar / Of thunderous waterfalls and torrents hoarse'[27] mixed with philosophical musing, take Coleridge:

it is a great Torrent from the Top of the Mountain to the Bottom . . . great Masses of Water, one after the other, that in twilight one might have feelingly compared them to a vast crowd of huge white Bears, rushing, one over the other, against the wind . . . The remainder of the Torrent is marked out by three great Waterfalls. . . . The middle . . . formed in this furious Rain one great *Waterwheel* endlessly revolving . . .—the third & highest is a mighty one indeed . . . is indeed so fearfully savage, & black, & jagged, that it tears the flood to pieces. . . . What a sight it is to look down on such a Cataract!—the wheels, that circumvolve in it—the leaping up & plunging forward of that infinity of Pearls & Glass Bulbs—the continual *change* of the *Matter*, the perpetual *Sameness* of the *Form*—it is an awful Image & Shadow of God & the World.[28]

Alongside the cataract-philosophizing of Coleridge we may place that of Senancour:

The great volume of water fell from a height of about three hundred feet. I crept as close to it as possible, and in a moment was drenched. . . . But I felt a return of my early emotions, as I was bathed in the leaping spray which flings its foam toward the clouds, as I heard the raging howl of the cataract whose waters have their birth in the silent ice, flow unceasingly from an unmoving source, are lost, and endlessly lost, with tumultuous roar. They plunge into chasms that they

[26] S. T. Coleridge, *Hints Towards the Formation of a More Comprehensive Theory of Life*, ed. Seth B. Watson (London: John Churchill, 1848), 31–2.
[27] Keats, *Poems*, 341.   [28] Coleridge, *Letters*, ii. 456–7. 25 Aug. 1802.

hollow out, and are forever falling in their eternal fall. Even such is the downward flow of the years and the centuries of man.

Further on in the passage the cataract is called 'the perpetual emblem of an unknown force, the singular and mysterious expression of the energy of the world':

> That icy water, restless, all-invading, filled with the spirit of motion, that majestic tumult of a leaping torrent, that mist forever flinging its billows into the air, swept away the forgetfulness into which years of stress and struggle had plunged me. . . . I seemed engulfed by the waters and living in the abyss. I had quit the earth; I looked back upon my life and it seemed ridiculous in my eyes; it filled me with pity.[29]

Chateaubriand, again, repeatedly witnesses the Romantic pre-occupation with torrents and cataracts. In the following passage about Niagara he does not draw explicit philosophical conclusions, as do Coleridge and Senancour (although he does so elsewhere); rather he suggests them by augmenting the sublimity of the cataract much as Shelley augments the sublimity of Mont Blanc:

> Soon we reached the edge of the cataract, whose mighty roar could be heard from afar. . . . The mass of water hurtling down in the south curves into a vast cylinder, then straightens into a snowy sheet, sparkling iridiscent in the sunlight. The eastern branch falls in dismal gloom, calling to mind some downpour of the great flood. A thousand rainbows arch and intersect over the abyss. As it strikes the shuddering rock, the water bounds back in foaming whirlpools, which drift up over the forest like the smoke of some vast conflagration. The scene is ornate with pine and wild walnut trees and rocks carved out in weird shapes. Eagles, drawn by air currents, spiral down into the depths of the chasm, and wolverines dangle by their supple tails from the ends of low-hanging branches, snatching the shattered corpses of elk and bears out of the abyss.[30]

As with torrents and cataracts, so with rivers and streams. From a dazzling cornucopia of possible examples, we may select a single one, this from Wordsworth:

> Never did a child stand by the side of a running stream, pondering within himself what power was the feeder of the perpetual current, from what never-wearied sources the body of water was supplied, but he must have been inevitably propelled to follow this question by another: 'Towards what abyss is it in progress? what receptacle can contain the mighty influx?' And the spirit of the answer must have been, though the word might be sea or ocean, accompanied perhaps with an image gathered from a map, or from the real object in

---

[29] *Senancour*, iii. 211–12.   [30] *Chateaubriand*, i. 74–5.

nature—these might have been the *letter*, but the *spirit* of the answer must have been *as* inevitably,—a receptacle without bounds or dimensions;—nothing less than infinity.[31]

Wordsworth's invocation of infinity points us to another major criterion of the Romantic sensibility. Infinity's symbol, the sea or the ocean, is no less omnipresent in Romantic literature than is process's symbol, the flowing stream or cataract; and infinity itself is an especially idiosyncratic and important Romantic emphasis. It is everywhere.[32] T. E. Hulme, indeed, in his twentieth-century attack on Romanticism, renders oblique homage to its ubiquity:

> You might say if you wished that the whole of the romantic attitude seems to crystallize in verse round metaphors of flight. Hugo is always flying, flying over abysses, flying up into the eternal gases. The word infinite in every other line. . . . I object even to the best of the romantics. . . . They cannot see that accurate description is a legitimate object of verse. Verse to them always means a bringing in of some of the emotions that are grouped round the word 'infinite'.[33]

As to why 'the word "infinite"' should be 'in every other line', or verse to the Romantics 'always mean a bringing in of some of the emotions that are grouped round the word "infinite"', we might rather Delphically avail ourselves of four statements by the scholar Fritz Strich. 'The Romantic Ideal must infinitely remain ideal, and all Romanticism is only a path and a way (*nur Weg und Bahn*).' 'Longing (*Sehnsucht*) is not the consequence, but rather the fundamental principle, the true basic concept of Romanticism.' Yet, because Romanticism is always 'only a path and a way', 'Die Seele der Romantik war die Sehnsucht ohne Ziel und Grenze und Gegenstand'—'the soul of Romanticism was longing without goal and boundary and object.' Accordingly, 'Die Sehnsucht der Romantik aber hat, wenn man hier noch von Ziel sprechen darf, ein unendliches Ziel: es liegt nicht nur in der Unendlichkeit, sondern es ist sie selbst'—'the longing of Romanticism has, if one may still speak of a goal, an infinite goal: the goal not only lies in infinity, but is infinity itself.'[34] In short, to use Byron's words from *Childe Harold*, the

---

[31] Wordsworth, *Prose*, ii. 51.

[32] Uhland even made the sense of the infinite equivalent to Romanticism as such: 'dies Ahnen des Unendlichen in den Anschauungen ist das Romantische'—'this presentiment of the infinite in what we see is Romanticism' (*Uhland*, ii. 348).

[33] T. E. Hulme, *Speculations: Essays on Humanism and the Philosophy of Art*, ed. Herbert Read (London: Routledge & Kegan Paul, 1949 [1924]), 120, 126–7.

[34] Fritz Strich, *Deutsche Klassik und Romantik, oder, Vollendung und Unendlichkeit. Ein Vergleich*, 3rd ed. (Munich: Meyer & Jessen, 1928), 10, 69, 107, 70.

Romantics in their most typical orientation were 'wanderers o'er Eternity / Whose bark drives on and on, and anchored ne'er shall be.'[35] What all this means is that the replacement of substance by function, with the attendant hegemony of process, results in unending change that constitutes an infinite series of displacements of meaning. Accordingly, Friedrich Schlegel defines 'Romantic poetry' as 'a progressive universal poetry' that can 'eternally only be in process of becoming' and 'can never be completed'.[36] In this matrix, to utilize a good English example (though the passage speaks not of poetry but of the normative Romantic preoccupation with external nature), Coleridge says:

I can contemplate nothing but parts, & parts are all *little*—!—My mind feels as if it ached to behold & know something *great*—something *one* & *indivisible*—and it is only in the faith of this that rocks or waterfalls, mountains or caverns give me the sense of sublimity or majesty!—But in this faith *all things* counterfeit infinity![37]

Another version of the Romantic apotheosis of process was supplied by a pervasive fascination with the nature and growth of vegetable organisms. Though the necessary slowness of such growth, especially as contrasted with the movement of streams, makes the analogy of organism and process not quite so obvious as that of currents and process, organism too led towards the unreached vistas symbolized by the infinite and eternal:

I feel an awe [wrote Coleridge] . . . whether I contemplate a single tree or flower, or meditate on vegetation throughout the world, as one of the great organs of the life of nature. Lo!—with the rising sun it commences its outward life and enters into open communion with all the elements. . . . At the same moment it strikes its roots and unfolds its leaves, absorbs and respires, steams forth its cooling vapour and finer fragrance. . . . Lo!—at the touch of light how it returns an air akin to light, and yet with the same pulse effectuates its own secret growth. . . . Lo!—how upholding the ceaseless plastic motion of the parts in the profoundest rest of the whole it becomes the visible organismus of the whole *silent* or *elementary* life of nature and, therefore, in incorporating the one extreme becomes the symbol of the other; the natural symbol of that higher life of reason, in which the whole series (known to us in our present state of being) is perfected, in which, therefore, all the subordinate gradations recur, and are re-ordained '*in more abundant honor*'. We had seen each in its own cast, and we now recognize them all as co-existing in the unity of a higher form, the Crown and Completion of the Earthly, and the Mediator of a new and heavenly series. Thus finally, the

---

[35] Byron, *Childe Harold*, Canto iii, ll. 669–70. [36] *Schlegel*, ii. 182.
[37] Coleridge, *Letters*, i. 349. 14 Oct. 1797.

vegetable creation, in the simplicity and uniformity of its *internal* structure
symbolizing the unity of nature, while it represents the omniformity of her
delegated functions in its *external* variety and manifoldedness, becomes the
record and chronicle of her ministerial acts, and inchases the vast unfolded
volume of the earth with the hieroglyphics of her history.[38]

If metaphors of organic growth, like metaphors of current, ultimately
lead into an infinity beyond our ken, organism also became the model for
a Romantic rejection of neoclassic literary canons defined by imitation,
decorum, genre, and by a general subscription to the concept of imposed
form. Ben Jonson, among the first annunciators of the neoclassic
sensibility, learned from his teacher, Camden, to write his poems
initially as prose statements and then cast them into poetic metres. Such
a technique was anathema to Romanticism. 'Versifying and rhyming are
very well,' said Shelley, 'but they don't constitute a poem. Any subject
that can be as well expressed in prose as verse is not poetry of a high
class.'[39] On the contrary, the poem should rise from within, following its
own inner laws, precisely on the analogy of a vegetable organism.
'Nature is organic,' wrote Friedrich Schlegel, 'and the highest beauty is
therefore eternally and always plantlike (*vegetabilisch*).'[40] 'If Poetry come
not as naturally as the Leaves to a tree it had better not come at all', said
Keats.[41]

These insistences resulted in the Romantic doctrine of organic form,
of which there are few better formulations than that of Coleridge:
'Remember that there is a difference between form as proceeding, and
shape as superinduced;—the latter is either the death or the imprison-
ment of the thing;—the former is its self-witnessing and self-effected
sphere of agency.'[42] Elsewhere, warning against 'confounding mechanical regularity with organic form', he appropriates almost verbatim a
formula by a 'continental critic', Wilhelm Schlegel:

The form is mechanic when on any given material we impress a predetermined
form, not necessarily arising out of the properties of the material, as when to a
mass of wet clay we give whatever shape we wish it to retain when hardened. The
organic form, on the other hand, is innate; it shapes as it develops itself from
within, and the fullness of its development is one and the same with the

[38] *The Collected Works of Samuel Taylor Coleridge. 6. Lay Sermons*, ed. R.J. White
(Princeton: Princeton University Press, 1972), 72–3.
[39] Trelawny, 75.   [40] *Schlegel*, ii. 264.   [41] Keats, *Letters*, i. 238. 27 Feb. 1818.
[42] Coleridge, 'On Poesy or Art', in *Biographia Literaria*, edited with his Aesthetical
Essays by J. Shawcross (London: Oxford University Press, 1907), ii. 262.

perfection of its outward form. Such is the life, such the form. Nature, the prime genial artist, inexhaustible in diverse powers, is equally inexhaustible in forms. Each exterior is the physiognomy of the being within, its true image reflected and thrown out from the concave mirror.[43]

Still another Romantic criterion, as we can see by referring to the first passage from Coleridge cited above to illustrate the Romantic fascination with the process of organism, is that of the symbol. Such an emphasis coincided with the emphasis on the unattainable infinite: 'Symbol', wrote Goethe, 'transfers the appearance into the idea, the idea into an image, in such a way that the idea remains always infinitely active and unattainable, and, even if expressed in all languages, remains in fact inexpressible.'[44]

At this point, if we peruse again the criteria noted so far, we see that, in addition to the characteristics emphasized by Hazlitt, no fewer than fifteen hallmarks of Romanticism have been identified: external nature, imagination, egotism, love of the particular, flight into the medieval, flight into the Orient, flight into drugs, a preoccupation with dreams, with melancholy, solitude, suicide, an ubiquitous awareness of process and current, a longing for the infinite and unattainable, an omnipresent involvement with the organic, and a profound commitment to symbol. Still more could be added; for instance, in a volume called *Romanticism and the Forms of Ruin*, I emphasized what I called the 'diasparactive triad' of 'incompleteness, fragmentation, and ruin' as essential determinants of the Romantic sensibility.[45]

But though more criteria could be isolated, for our purposes here it suffices merely to have a goodly number. René Wellek, in a classic essay in which he seeks to unify the determinants of Romanticism, reduces them to three: 'imagination for the view of poetry, nature for the view of the world, and symbol and myth for poetic style.'[46] But in this reduction he falls, as it were, between two stools. On the one hand, even in terms of the listing just cited, Wellek's three criteria do not encompass enough of Romanticism's characteristics to give us a reliable feeling of the contour

[43] Samuel Taylor Coleridge, *Shakespearean Criticism*, ed. Thomas Middleton Raysor, Everyman's Library (London: Dent; New York: Dutton, 1960), i. 198.

[44] *Goethe*, ix. 532.

[45] Thomas McFarland, *Romanticism and the Forms of Ruin: Wordsworth, Coleridge, and Modalities of Fragmentation* (Princeton: Princeton University Press, 1981), e.g. 5–50.

[46] René Wellek, 'The Concept of Romanticism in Literary History', *Concepts of Criticism* (New Haven: Yale University Press, 1963), 128–98. The formula, 'imagination for the view of poetry, nature for the view of the world, and symbol and myth for poetic style' appears on page 161.

of that sensibility, and on the other hand, the number of three is still too large to claim unification.

The seeming heterogeneity of characteristics has indeed always posed a problem for the definition of the Romantic sensibility. In the 1920s the historian of ideas, A. O. Lovejoy, in a notorious essay called 'On the Discrimination of Romanticisms', argued that we should give up the search for such a general entity as Romanticism and content ourselves with dealing with individual characteristics as they arose: 'any attempt at a *general* appraisal even of a single chronologically determinate Romanticism—still more, of "Romanticism" as a whole—is a fatuity.'[47] He was not able to explain, however, how one accounted for the intuitive applicability of the class name, Romanticism, for the varieties he sought to discriminate. An oak, we realize, is different from a linden, a linden from a sycamore, a sycamore from a maple, but at the very moment we recognize the differences, we realize that the fact that we call all four 'trees' indicates a sameness that transcends the differences. That we recognize intuitively that various characteristics indicate 'Romanticism' is the best warrant for the existence of such a spirit of the age. That we find it difficult then to say exactly what constitutes Romanticism is a perplexity only less universal but no more alarming than that confessed by Augustine: 'What then is time? If no one asks me I know; if I wish to explain it to one that asks, I know not.'[48] We all function in time, whether we can explain it or not; almost any scholar who works in the Romantic movement comes to know the 'feel' of Romanticism, whether or not he can formulate the sensibility in unified terms.

An analogy would be the difficulties in attempting to understand some game—bridge, let us say—simply by inspecting the rules. Anyone who plays bridge understands the unity of the game; only those who approached it without living experience of the game would find it heterogeneous. It is complex, yes; heterogeneous, no. We can imagine some Lovejoy of the bridge books arguing that because a finesse is different from a slam convention, a forcing two bid quite unlike a one no-trump response, there is no such thing as bridge, and we should content ourselves merely with collecting various characteristics under that name. Most commentators, on the contrary, do realize that there is a spirit of the age called Romanticism; indeed, one may point to M. H.

---

[47] Arthur O. Lovejoy, 'On the Discrimination of Romanticisms', [1924], *Essays in the History of Ideas* (Baltimore: The Johns Hopkins Press, 1948), 252.

[48] Augustine, *Confessions*, xi. 14.

Abrams's article entitled 'English Romanticism: The Spirit of the Age'.[49]

Perhaps a more useful, or at least a more versatile, analogy for the special problems of the epoch could be drawn from objects the Romantics themselves loved. Think of Romanticism as a mountain range, its various characteristics, and, alternatively, its various individuals, as the different peaks in that range. Thus process might well be thought of as the Everest of Romanticism, external nature as the K2, imagination as the Kanchenjunga, organism as the Annapurna, melancholy as the Dhaulagiri, medievalism as the Nanga Parbat, and so on. The range would look different from different perspectives. Approaching from the south through Nepal one would see high peaks; approaching from the west through Delhi, Everest would not be visible at all. From far enough away, say from Eastern India, one would see not the great peaks but only foothills. A Lovejoy of mountaineering might argue that because of the different views that exist, there was no such thing as the Himalayas, and that we should merely record the various mountains. Only those with intimate travelling experience in the area, or in a position to overfly it, could testify that indeed there was a range, not merely individual mountains.

Such an image is particularly appropriate for the concerns of this book. For in dealing with three established figures in English literature of the early nineteenth century, Lamb, Hazlitt, and De Quincey, the book will insist throughout that they be viewed as mountains in the Romantic range. They have in previous commentaries largely been seen as isolated monadnocks, but in fact they are parts of the great range. To understand this truth will be both to bring them back into our ken as more serious figures in terms of the dominant sensibility of their time, and also to add further mapping to Romanticism itself. Lamb, Hazlitt, and De Quincey are very substantial figures, not dizzying elevations like Wordsworth and Coleridge, perhaps, but definitely mountains, not outlying hills.

To take them merely as hills is both to lose perspective on their own elevation and to lose sight of the Romantic range. Indeed, when viewing Romanticism merely through its outlying foothills, not seeing its snow-capped peaks, one can easily conclude that there are no snow-capped

[49] M. H. Abrams, 'English Romanticism: The Spirit of the Age', *The Correspondent Breeze: Essays on English Romanticism* (New York: W. W. Norton & Company, 1984), 44–75.

peaks and that indeed the report of a range is false. A recent book by Marilyn Butler does not see any Romantic range at all:

> We began with the received view that at some time at the end of the eighteenth century a Romantic Revolution occurred, which worked a permanent change in literature and in the other arts, and scored a decisive victory over the classicism which was there before. In reality there would seem to have been no one battle and no complete victory. It is not even clear that there were defeats.[50]

Such a view heralds the revival of Lovejoy's opinion. 'As for the other received notions about English Romanticism,' continues Butler,

> some of these are too hard to reconcile with the conclusions just summarized.... [T]he preceding chapters have tended to highlight differences rather than common ground between the writers. The impression left is hardly of a closely coherent body of feeling.
>
> 'Romanticism' is inchoate because it is not a single intellectual movement but a complex of responses to certain conditions which Western society has experienced and continued to experience since the middle of the eighteenth century'.... Perhaps the best of all reasons for shedding preconceptions about Romanticism is not the point of principle—that they may be untrue—but the point of pragmatism—that they interfere with so much good reading. How many students have puzzled themselves into antipathy, trying to fathom what the Lyrical Ballads initiated; or what the common denominator may be in various writers' attitudes to the self, to God, or to Nature; or precisely why Shelley, Scott and Byron must be said to be Romantic?[51]

But Marilyn Butler throughout her career has been involved only in the foothills of Romanticism. Not only does her book reveal little or no concern for the German, French, and other continental peaks in the range, and not much more for the secondary elucidations that have accumulated around the idea of Romanticism, but she herself has comprehensively mapped only the foothills. Her earlier books were on Maria Edgeworth, Thomas Love Peacock, and Jane Austen, two of them foothills, one a major peak but a true monadnock in terms of any definition of the Romantic sensibility that has ever been offered. Such a traverse does not go into the heart of the Romantic range and can readily lead to the conclusion that no range exists.

For instance, Marilyn Butler's most successful book is perhaps her volume on Peacock, and Peacock virtually made a career of anti-Romantic sentiment. One thinks not only of his satirical animadversions

---

[50] Marilyn Butler, *Romantics, Rebels and Reactionaries. English Literature and its Background 1760–1830* (Oxford: Oxford University Press, 1981), 183.
[51] Ibid. 183–4, 187.

in *Sir Proteus*, in *Melincourt* (with its visit to 'the poeticopolitical, rhapsodicoprosaical, deisidæmoniacoparadoxographical, pseudolatreiological, transcendental meteorosophist, Moley Mystic, Esquire, of Cimmerian Lodge',[52] who is a rather delightful rendering of Coleridge), and in *Nightmare Abbey*; but especially in *The Four Ages of Poetry*. This essay, which I regard as both more serious and more profound than received opinion would have it, is not only anti-Romantical in tone and viewpoint, but contains a specific and scathing attack on the Lake Poets, one that might instructively be compared with the long passage by Hazlitt quoted at the beginning of this chapter. Peacock represents some modern poets, 'patriarchs of the age of brass', as ratiocinating in the following manner: 'Poetical genius is the finest of all things, and we feel that we have more of it than any one ever had. The way to bring it to perfection is to cultivate poetical impressions exclusively. Poetical impressions can be received only among natural scenes: for all that is artificial is anti-poetical. Society is artificial, therefore we will live out of society. The mountains are natural, therefore we will live in the mountains. There we shall be shining models of purity and virtue, passing the whole day in the innocent and amiable occupation of going up and down hill, receiving poetical impressions, and communicating them in immortal verse to admiring generations.'[53] He· then acidly reflects on the passage: 'To some such perversion of intellect we owe that egregious confraternity of rhymesters, known by the name of the Lake Poets. . . . They wrote verses on a new principle; saw rocks and rivers in a new light; and remaining studiously ignorant of history, society, and human nature, cultivated the phantasy only at the expense of the memory and the reason; and contrived, though they had retreated from the world for the express purpose of seeing nature as she was, to see her only as she was not, converting the land they lived in into a sort of fairy-land, which they peopled with mysticisms and chimæras. This gave what is called a new tone to poetry, and conjured up a herd of desperate imitators . . .'[54] He continues with sharp thrusts at the chief Romantics: 'While the historian and the philosopher are advancing in, and accelerating, the progress of knowledge, the poet is wallowing in the rubbish of departed ignorance, and raking up the ashes of dead savages to find gewgaws and rattles for the grown babies of the age. Mr Scott digs up the poachers and cattle-stealers of the ancient border. Lord Byron cruizes for thieves and pirates on the shores of the Morea and

[52] *Peacock*, ii. 328.   [53] Ibid. iii. 17–18.   [54] Ibid. 18.

among the Greek Islands. Mr Southey wades through ponderous volumes of travels and old chronicles, from which he carefully selects all that is false, useless, and absurd, as being essentially poetical; and when he has a commonplace book full of monstrosities, strings them into an epic. Mr Wordsworth picks up village legends from old women and sextons; and Mr Coleridge . . . superadds the dreams of crazy theologians and the mysticisms of German metaphysics, and favours the world with visions in verse . . .'[55]

Yet even in his career of attacking Romanticism, Peacock not only recognizes the unity of the Romantic but necessarily attaches his literary fortunes to it. He supplied Shelley with the ultra-Romantic title of 'Alastor, or, the Spirit of Solitude'; more importantly, the passages just quoted delineate, though in negative light, important features of Romanticism.

No writer, in short, really can escape the spirit of his age, and with this realization we are only mildly surprised to find that the youthful Peacock, before he embarked on his satiric career, availed himself of Romantic meditations on ruins in *Palmyra*, and of Romantic melancholy in *The Philosophy of Melancholy*; nor are we much surprised when in 1808 he writes to a Romantically questing friend in the high idiom of Romanticism: 'You went over the same ground on which I wandered alone in the autumn of 1806. . . . Did you visit the banks of the sweet silver Teviot, and that most lovely of rivers, the undescribably-fascinating Tweed? Did you sit by moonlight in the ruins of Melrose? Did you stand by twilight in that romantic wood which overhangs the Teviot, on the site of Roxburgh Castle?'[56]

Romanticism permeates even Peacock's satiric work. Thus, for only one instance, a chapter in *Melincourt* called, with Romantic directness, 'The Torrent', takes note of 'the romantic chasm, bright in its bed of rocks, chequered by pale sunbeams through the leaves of the ash;'[57] and a character stands 'gazing on the torrent with awful delight. The contemplation of the mighty energies of nature, which nothing could resist or impede, absorbed, for a time, all considerations of the difficulty of regaining her home. . . . She was roused from her reverie only by the sound of its dissolution. She looked back, and found herself on the solitary rock insulated by the swelling flood.'[58]

The Romantic range, one must reiterate, indubitably does exist; its

---

[55] Ibid. 19–20.
[56] *Peacock*, viii. 161–2.
[57] Ibid. ii. 105.   [58] Ibid. 104.

peaks and elevations, and even, as with Peacock, its foothills, are all interconnected. It was noted above that De Quincey summons three discrete Romantic *topoi*—orientalism, dreams, and drugs—in one of his characteristic passages; that Coleridge summons process and symbol and organism and nature in another passage. Such alignments constantly recur in Romantic practice. Drug-taking and the infinite, for instance, would seem to be so widely separated that they could have no likely common pertinence; yet Baudelaire sees them as inextricably interlinked:

Alas! Man's vices, as filled with horror as they are thought to be, contain the proof (if only in their infinite spread!) of man's craving for infinity; only, it is a craving that often takes the wrong road. . . . This visible lord of visible nature (I am speaking of man), has sought to create Paradise through pharmacy, and through fermented beverages, like some maniac who would replace solid furniture and real gardens with scenery painted on canvas and mounted on a frame. In my opinion, it is in this corruption of the meaning of infinity that lies the reason for all sinful intemperance, from the . . . intoxication of a certain literary man . . . in opium . . . to the lowest, most repugnant drunk that rolls in the filth of the gutter, his brain afire.[59]

The criterion of the infinite, again, and to note a diverging alignment, combines readily with the criterion of solitude in Shelley's declaration that, 'I love all waste / And solitary places; where we taste / The pleasure of believing what we see / Is boundless, as we wish our souls to be.'[60]

If we seek for the factor that makes comprehensible the mutual affinities and continual recombinations of the varying phenomena of Romanticism, it is possible to elucidate that factor in terms of the metaphor of the mountain range already invoked. The Himalayas, we are told, were thrown up by vast geological pressures generated by the subcontinent of India moving northward in the Indian Ocean and colliding with the continental land mass of Asia. Such, *mutatis mutandis*, is the origin of Romantic phenomena. Romanticism is a series of direct responses and reaction formations to a gigantic and unprecedented crisis in European culture, one that threatened the securities of man's economic, social, and spiritual life, one that above all threatened the very values by which he thought himself significant. The effect of those pressures exists and has even been augmented today, and Romanticism is the true beginning of our modern world.

Both Romantic melancholy and Romantic egotism, to take two

---

[59] *Baudelaire*, i. 402–3.   [60] *Shelley*, ii. 179.

seemingly opposed criteria, can be seen as a response to those pressures, the first as a recognition of them, the second as a denial. Rousseau and Byron, in different ways, were agitating the sense of self because the meaning of self was threatened; when Fichte located all reality within the ego, the gesture was so directly the opposite of the experience of reality as to constitute a reaction formation to the true situation. Fichte, indeed, is the counterpart of denial that will inevitably accompany those forces that lead to the melancholy vision of Malthus, where the individual is drowned under exponential duplications.

In the same manner, the love of the medieval ('You know the Enchanted Castle,' wrote Keats in a poetical epistle, 'O Phoebus! that I had thy sacred word / To shew this Castle, in fair dreaming wise / Unto my friend, while sick and ill he lies!'),[61] the fascination with the oriental, the preoccupation with dreams and reverie, and the involvement with drugs were all versions of escape from a reality that had become intolerably threatening (more than a half-century ago Hoxie Neale Fairchild defined Romanticism as 'the endeavor, in the face of growing factual obstacles, to achieve, to retain, or to justify' what he called an 'illusioned view of the universe and of human life').[62] The Byronic hero is attractive in his defiance, though already under great pressure in his being: 'That livid cheek, that stony air / Of mix'd defiance and despair!'[63] But it is only a step from the splendour of Byron's Giaour to the worm-like existence of Dostoevsky's underground man, now buckled under those same pressures that the Byronic hero rejected in contempt.

What were these pressures? They were different in origin, but a unity in their effect. Whether they resulted in Promethean or Satanic defiance or in suicide, they threatened the very meaning of life. Socially they were signalized by the French Revolution, with its attendant shattering of age-old securities of class and status and theological assumption. Economically, they were signalized by the Industrial Revolution, which not only turned the cities and means of production into Satan's mills, and uprooted the populace from the traditional permanence of a farming life, but also called into question the very significance of individual craftsmanship; it dictated the emergence of that alienated labour so vividly described from Schiller through to Engels and Marx.

[61] Keats, *Poems*, 242.
[62] Hoxie Neale Fairchild, *The Romantic Quest* (New York: Columbia University Press, 1931), 251.
[63] Byron, *The Giaour; A Fragment of a Turkish Tale*, ll. 907–8.

Spiritually, they were signalized by the collapse of religion in the French Enlightenment, a collapse feared even where it was denied. The French Romantic, Nerval, in a poem in which he agonizedly said 'Dieu n'est pas! Dieu n'est plus!' invoked as epigraph the statement of the German Romantic, Jean Paul: 'God is dead! the heavens are empty.'[64] The English Romantic, Coleridge, wrote, in a poem about the meaning of human life if there were no immortality:

> If dead, we cease to be; if total gloom
> Swallow up life's brief flash for aye, we fare
> As summer-gusts, of sudden birth and doom
>
> .   .   .   .   .   .
>
> If even a soul like Milton's can know death;
> O Man! thou vessel purposeless, unmeant,
>
> .   .   .   .   .   .
>
> If rootless thus, thus substanceless thy state,
> Go weigh thy dreams . . .
>   Why rejoices
> Thy heart with hollow joy for hollow good?
> Why cowl thy face beneath the mourner's hood?
> Be sad! be glad! be neither! seek, or shun!
> Though hast no reason why![65]

Romanticism was a complex of realizations and denials set in motion by the fear that man had 'no reason why'. And underlying its three main sources of political-social, economic, and spiritual pressure was the single great transformation: the demise of substance and the rise of process. Carlyle's notable essay *Characteristics*, written in 1831, was an attempt to look process and its concomitant, incessant change, squarely in the eye without flinching:

Nevertheless so much has become evident to every one, that this wondrous Mankind is advancing somewhither; that at least all human things are, have been and forever will be, in Movement and Change.[66]

And he says soothingly that 'In change . . . there is nothing terrible . . . ; on the contrary, it lies in the very essence of our lot and life in this world.'[67] Hegel, the philosopher pre-eminent of Romanticism, for the traditional Being (*Sein*) of philosophical investigation (the word was a cognate of the Greek word for substance, *ousia*), substituted an idea of Being adulterated by Nothingness that resulted in Becoming (*Werden*)

[64] *Nerval*, i. 32.   [65] Coleridge, *Poems*, i. 425–6.   [66] *Carlyle*, xxviii. 37.
[67] Ibid. 39.

as the essence of all history and culture.[68] Goethe too accepted the new
hegemony of process and change. His Faust, musing on the text, 'In
the beginning was the Word', substituted 'In the beginning was the
Act'; declared that 'Nur rastlos betätigt sich der Mann'—'only restless
activity makes the man'; resolved 'Zum höchsten Dasein immerfort zu
streben'—'for highest existence henceforth to strive'; and believed that
'Wer immer strebend sich bemüht, / Den können wir erlösen'—'who
always busies himself with striving, / Him can we save.'[69]

But those who embraced the displacement of being by becoming, of
substance by process, were more than matched by those who were
shattered by the prospect of endless change. 'Mutations sans terme,' exclaimed Senancour's Oberman, aghast, 'action sans but, impénétrabilité
universelle; voilà ce qui nous est connu de ce monde où nous régnons.'
—'changes interminable, action without goal, universal opaqueness;
that is what we know of this world where we reign.'[70] Others reacted
with Romantic defences: with frantic egotism to deny the sense of a
substanceless state, with drugs, with retreat into dreams or reverie or
imagined realms: 'magic casements opening on the foam / Of perilous
seas in faery lands forlorn.'[71] The whole mighty range of Romanticism
was cast up by the still mightier but hidden forces exerted by the French
Revolution, by the Industrial Revolution, and by the collapse of religion,
and they in their turn by the still vaster conversion of ideas of substance
to those of a process that moved remorselessly towards a nihilism of all
meaning. 'Les mois changent,' said Oberman, 'les années se succèdent;
tout se renouvelle en vain. . . . Au milieu de ce que j'ai desiré, tout me
manque; je n'ai rien obtenu, je ne possède rien: l'ennui consume ma
durée dans un long silence'—'the months change, the years succeed
one another, everything renews itself in vain. . . . Amid that which I have
desired, everything is lacking to me; I have obtained nothing, I possess
nothing: ennui consumes my duration in a long silence.'[72]

---

[68] e.g., 'Das reine Sein und das reine Nichts ist also dasselbe. Was die Wahrheit ist, ist weder
das Sein noch das Nichts, sondern daß das Sein in Nichts und das Nichts in Sein—nicht
übergeht, sondern übergangen ist. Aber ebensosehr ist die Wahrheit nicht ihre Ununter-
schiedenheit, sondern daß sie nicht dasselbe, daß sie absolut unterschieden, aber ebenso
ungetrennt und untrennbar sind und unmittelbar jedes in seinem Gegenteil verschwindet.
Ihre Wahrheit ist also dies Bewegung des unmittelbaren Verschwindens des einen in dem
anderen: das Werden' (Hegel, v. 83).   [69] Goethe, v. 181, 195, 293, 520.
[70] Senancour, iii. 168.   [71] Keats, Poems, 371.
[72] Senancour, iii. 166. Again: 'le vide creusa mon coeur; des besoins sans bornes me
consumèrent dans le silence, et l'ennui de la vie fut mon seul sentiment dans l'âge où
l'on commence à vivre' 168.

All aspects of Romanticism respond to the test of these pressures. To the fifteen characteristics isolated above, to the others supplied by Hazlitt or by reference to my own work, we may add still more and find that they too respond to the conception of pressure on the 'reason why' of human existence. For instance, two widespread criteria of Romanticism not previously discussed are wanderlust and madness. The Austrian Romantic poet, Lenau, to give just one example, journeyed from Austria to, of all places, Bucyrus, Ohio, returned to Austria, and went mad. His madness was a direct witness to the pressures of existence; his frantic, futile, and entirely typical Romantic 'quest' an indirect one.[73]

We look at Romanticism and see a seemingly joyous Wordsworth, but have to be taught by modern Wordsworthian criticism how racked his existence actually was. We look at others, and the pressure on their substanceless state is vividly apparent. In just a few pages, Trelawny manages to record that in response to a statement about Byron's diet, 'but if you wish to live—', Byron replied, 'Who wants to live? Not I';[74] and that Byron said 'nothing is certain, and so he believes nothing.'[75] (Byron, insists Trelawny again, 'believed in nothing.')[76] Within a few more pages Trelawny says that,

an old fellow pointed with his stick to a hat, books, and loose papers lying about, and then to a deep pool of dark glimmering water, saying 'Eccolo!' I thought he meant that Shelley was in or under the water. The careless, not to say impatient, way in which the Poet bore his burden of life, caused a vague dread amongst his family and friends that he might lose or cast it away at any moment.[77]

And a few pages later Shelley is quoted as saying, 'Mine is a life of failures.'[78] As Carlyle sombrely notes:

Behold a Byron, in melodious tones, 'cursing his day': he mistakes earth-born passionate Desire for heaven-inspired Freewill; without heavenly loadstar, rushes madly into the dance of meteoric lights that hover on the mad Mahlstrom; and goes down among its eddies. Hear a Shelley filling the earth with inarticulate wail; like the infinite, inarticulate grief and weeping of forsaken infants. A noble Friedrich Schlegel, stupefied in that fearful loneliness, as of a silenced battle-field, flies back to Catholicism; as a child might to its slain

---

[73] Romantic wanderlust, at least in its societal manifestations, was a visible image of the dominance of change in the Romantic era no less than a premonitory signal for our modern situation. 'Keep moving!' wrote Coleridge in some sardonic lines of 1824, 'Steam, or Gas, or Stage, / Hold, cabin, steerage, hencoop's cage— / Tour, Journey, Voyage, Lounge, Ride, Walk, / Skim, Sketch, Excursion, Travel-talk— / For move you must! 'Tis now the rage, / The law and fashion of the Age.'   [74] Trelawny, 98.
[75] Ibid. 100.   [76] Ibid. 104.   [77] Ibid. 113.   [78] Ibid. 131.

mother's bosom, and clings there. In lower regions, how many a poor Hazlitt must wander on God's verdant earth, like the Unblest on burning deserts; passionately dig wells, and draw up only the dry quicksand; believe that he is seeking Truth, yet only wrestle among endless Sophisms, doing desperate battle as with spectre-hosts; and die and make no sign![79]

Carlyle's inclusion of Hazlitt—though 'in lower regions'—among the agonized great ones of Romanticism is entirely just, and it makes a fitting transition to the special concerns of this volume. Throughout its various statements, this book will constantly see the brilliant essayists, Lamb, Hazlitt, and De Quincey, as Romantic figures, and by that token as figures under stress. Each took his cross and bore it towards his individual destiny. Their own elevations, as serene as others occupying our view of the great range, were like all the others actually cast up by gigantic pressures that tormented the clay and shingle of ordinary human experience. Furthermore, all three will be aligned so that their perspective takes in the snow-capped peak of Coleridge, itself a notable testament to those rending pressures of existence that had become so mightily enhanced in the Romantic period.

But a final transumption of metaphor is required to conclude this preliminary meditation. In this metalepsis, the book might be thought of as a kind of extended composition for piano. The part for the right hand weaves variations on the characteristics of Romanticism as seen in the lives and achievements of the three essayists. The left hand maintains the bass burden, through varying figures, of the influence of Coleridge on all three lives and their works. The parts for both right and left hands, in all three movements, eventuate in a single composition that honours the struggle of all its thematic participants, of Coleridge, of Charles Lamb, of William Hazlitt, and of Thomas De Quincey.

[79] *Carlyle*, xxviii. 31–2.

2

Charles Lamb and the Politics of Survival

THE reputation of Charles Lamb does not stand as high as it once did. For instance, Geoffrey Tillotson in 1962 felt obliged, in his introduction to the Everyman edition of *The Essays of Elia*, to mount a defence against what he termed 'the so-called "faults" of Lamb, his facetiousness, whimsicality and sentimentality'.[1] A half century or so earlier, however, in 1906, William Ernest Henley, in a preface to an Everyman volume of Hazlitt, could write that 'as a critic of letters', Hazlitt 'lacks the intense, immortalizing vision, even as he lacks, in places, the illuminating and inevitable style of Lamb'.[2] Henley went on to make a fuller comparison:

As a writer, therefore, it is with Lamb that I would bracket [Hazlitt]: they are dissimilars, but they go gallantly and naturally together. . . . Give us these two, with some ripe Cobbett, a volume of Southey, some Wordsworth, certain pages of Shelley, a great deal of the Byron who wrote letters, and we get the right prose of the time. The best of it all, perhaps, is the best of Lamb. But Hazlitt's, for different qualities, is so imminent and shining a second that I hesitate as to the pre-eminency. Probably the race is Lamb's.[3]

Henley's preference hardly obtains at present. Not only would almost everyone now think of Hazlitt as the more significant figure, and certainly the more distinguished prose stylist, but, perhaps more importantly, Lamb simply does not *interest* very many intellectuals today. We think of David Bromwich's recent laudatory assessment of Hazlitt's achievement, or we think of Borges's testimonials to his urgent debt to De Quincey; for the tradition of Lamb we probably can look no higher than the Christopher Morleys of the world, twinkly, pipe-smoking, fireside-sitting.

It will be argued in this chapter that Lamb is a more serious cultural figure than we are accustomed to realize, a deeper, more interesting, and above all more iconic one. What has happened to generate the prevailing view, one surmises, is that we simply concede Lamb's charm, his

---

[1] Geoffrey Tillotson, 'Introduction' to Charles Lamb, *Essays of Elia*, Everyman's Library (London: Dent; New York: Dutton, 1962), p. xiv.
[2] Henley, p. viii.   [3] Ibid. pp. viii–ix.

inimitable humour, and his whimsy, but then use those features of his work and personality as a curtain that we drape over his activity, much as we put sheets over our furniture when we are going to leave the house untended for a lengthy period. The insistence here, on the contrary, is that we should not look at Lamb through the obscuring veil of his whimsy, but rather look at the whimsy in the context of Lamb's larger situation as an exemplar of the Romantic movement. Lamb may seem to lack depth when we view him through the hazy shimmer of his charm; when we look at the charm from the perspective of Lamb's situation, however, we see it as arising from the abyss.

It is of the abyss that these three concluding statements in a letter of 1800 testify: 'I am completely shipwreck'd.—My head is quite bad . . . I almost wish that Mary were dead . . .'[4] The unflagging humour, the relentless whimsy, the herculean outlay of charm, fortifications watchfully manned throughout a lifetime, were designed to defend him, in the daily round of existence, from the stark realization of the smothering burden that Mary placed on his possibilities for happiness.

The statements, indeed, come at the end of a letter to Coleridge that speaks of a situation so bizarre in its horror, that we may take it as our 'representative anecdote'—I borrow the conception from Kenneth Burke—for what was really going on in Lamb's life, and for which the charm, in his personal relationships as well as in his writing, constituted nothing less than a politics of survival. 'I don't know why I write', writes Lamb in vain to his clay-footed idol,

except from the propensity misery has to tell her griefs.—Hetty died on Friday night, about 11 O clock, after 8 days illness. Mary in consequence of fatigue and anxiety is fallen ill again, and I was obliged to remove her yesterday.—I am left alone in a house with nothing but Hetty's dead body to keep me company. . . . Tomorrow I bury her, and then I shall be quite alone, with nothing but a cat, to remind me that the house has been full of living beings like myself.—My heart is quite sunk, and I don't know where to look for relief—. Mary will get better again, but her constantly being liable to such relapses is dreadful,—nor is it the least of our Evils, that her case & all our story is so well known around us . . . We are in a manner *marked*.—Excuse my troubling you, but I have nobody by me to speak to.[5]

The 'excuse my troubling you' is pure Lamb, a forming film of the ingratiating cover that iced over the bottomless depths into which his heart had sunk. The ingratiating cover was impenetrable in Lamb. The

---

[4] Lamb, *Letters*, i. 203.   [5] Ibid. 202.

great-souled Chekhov was drinking champagne with his wife when he suddenly announced, 'I am dying', and died. We can imagine that Lamb, in the same situation, tippling with a dream-wife, would say, 'Excuse me, I am dying'. But the situation in the representative anecdote, as in Lamb's life, gets still worse. Even the corpse of Hetty is human company, but tomorrow brings the quite alone—'quite alone, with nothing but a cat'. Mary, of course, did get better; her brother crept along, chained like Ixion to the ledgers of the East India Company, towards alcoholism and death.[6] But Mary survived, and survived, and survived. 'Mary Lamb, I rejoice to say,' noted Crabb Robinson in 1837, three years after Charles's death, 'has been long in quiet good health. She shewed me her brother's grave a few days ago with composure and something like cheerfulness.'[7]

However alone Lamb might have been in his inner life, that very loneliness and desolation accredit him as an iconic figure for the Romantic situation. Indeed, if we consider Lamb in the general matrix of Romanticism and its criteria, we shall see him more clearly, even when he does not on the surface appear to conform to those criteria, that if we think of him as merely an English essayist. To that end, we must invoke at further length those defining characteristics of Romanticism broached in the previous chapter.

The seemingly heterogeneous characteristics of Romanticism have, as noted in the previous chapter, led some commentators, from A. O. Lovejoy to Marilyn Butler, to doubt the very existence of a Romantic essence. Others, such as Earl Wasserman and M. H. Abrams, while not denying the existence of Romanticism, have interpreted the phenomenon as representing much more optimism about the human condition than I think is justified. Abrams, for example, in attempting 'to decide

---

[6] For a survey (perhaps too ameliorative) of Lamb's drinking habits, see David Cecil, *A Portrait of Charles Lamb* (London: Constable, 1983), 122–6. For a more worried view of the matter see the repeated observations and private comments in Henry Crabb Robinson's diary. Cf. Carlyle's harsh portrait: 'Insuperable proclivity to gin in poor old Lamb. His talk contemptibly small, indicating wondrous ignorance and shallowness . . . screwed into frosty artificialities, ghastly make-believe of wit; in fact, more like "diluted insanity" (as I defined it) than anything of real jocosity, humor, or geniality.' (Carlyle, *Reminiscences*, 250). Again: '. . . a miserable, drink-besotted, spindle-shanked skeleton of a body' (Carlyle, *Letters*, v. 375). 'He was sinking into drink' (v. 448); 'clamours for "gin and water" with a rude barbarism . . .' (vi. 51).

[7] *Robinson*, iii. 853. Six years later, in 1843: 'We found her better than we feared. . . . Mary Lamb is eighty on the 3rd December next. She was in spirits, inquired after my brother, but talked rather ramblingly' (ii. 635).

what can properly be called Romantic', concludes, in his *Natural Supernaturalism*, that chief among their values 'were life, love, liberty, hope, and joy', that for them 'the norm of life is joy'.[8] My own *Romanticism and the Forms of Ruin*, on the contrary, stands, in the words of E. D. Hirsch, as 'a corrective to the general view of the romantics as the last of the happy, whole persons in Western tradition'.[9] Where Abrams sees joy as the norm, I see incompleteness, fragmentation, and ruin, although invocations of joy are frequently shored against that ruin.

For instance, one of Coleridge's stanzas seems whole-hearted in its commitment to joy:

> Joy, virtuous Lady! Joy that ne'er was given,
> Save to the pure, and in their purest hour,
> Life, and Life's effluence, cloud at once and shower,
> Joy, Lady! is the spirit and the power,
> Which wedding Nature to us gives in dower
> A new Earth and new Heaven,
> Undreamt of by the sensual and the proud—
> Joy is the sweet voice, Joy the luminous cloud—
> We in ourselves rejoice![10]

But this paroxysm of joy is merely an episode in a larger texture of sadness, is, in fact, part of a stanza in a poem called 'Dejection: an Ode', which speaks of a norm of 'dull pain', of 'a grief without a pang, void, dark, and drear'. Though the last word of the poem is 'rejoice', the words 'moan', 'groan', and 'scream' haunt the penultimate stanza; and the poem's largest context is a presence of pain: 'But now afflictions bow me down to earth.'

Wordsworth's repeated invocations of joy, too, as most modern commentators realize, can be seen as attempts to deny the contrary. As a single instance that I have pointed out elsewhere, Wordsworth's statement in the 'Immortality Ode', 'O joy! that in our embers / Is something that doth live', does not follow from the poem's logic, and might more logically be stated as 'Oh woe is me, that all my burning life is now reduced to embers'.[11] As I have said, 'To find the flame of life replaced

[8] M. H. Abrams, *Natural Supernaturalism: Tradition and Revolution in Romantic Literature* (New York: W. W. Norton & Company, Inc., 1971), 427, 431.
[9] E. D. Hirsch as quoted on the dust-jacket of Thomas McFarland, *Romanticism and the Forms of Ruin: Wordsworth, Coleridge, and Modalities of Fragmentation* (Princeton: Princeton University Press, 1981).   [10] Coleridge, *Poems*, i. 365–6.
[11] Thomas McFarland, 'Wordsworth on Man, on Nature, and on Human Life', *Studies in Romanticism*, 21 (Winter, 1982), 603.

by embers calls for gloom, not joy. The poem has moved bleakly enough from the idea that "Heaven lies about us in our infancy" to the idea that "Shades of the prison house begin to close / Upon the growing Boy", from the idea that though the boy still beholds the light, "At length the Man perceives it die away, / And fade into the light of common day." The logical burden of the poem, therefore, is depression at this loss of being, at the haunted sense that "The things which I have seen I now can see no more", at the certain knowledge "That there hath past away a glory from the earth".[12]

In short, it was not joy that was the Romantic norm, but melancholy, as commentators on the phenomenon as a European, rather than a merely English, cultural formation have always tended to realize. For instance, Mario Praz stresses in *The Romantic Agony* that 'there is no end to the examples which might be quoted from the Romantic and Decadent writers on the subject of [the] indissoluble union of the beautiful and the sad, on the supreme beauty of that beauty which is accursed.'[13] 'Mon existence,' wrote Flaubert in 1839, 'que j'avais rêvée si belle, si poétique, si large, si amoureuse, sera comme les autres monotone, sensée, bête. . . . Pauvre fou qui avait rêvé la gloire, l'amour, les lauriers, les voyages, l'Orient, que sais-je? Ce que le monde a de plus beau, modestement, je me l'étais donné d'avance. Mais tu n'auras comme les autres que de l'ennui pendant ta vie et une tombe après ta mort . . .'.[14] As a single additional example, another commentator, Richard Fargher, in noting that the eighteenth-century 'comte de Tilly exemplifies the development from *vide de l'âme* to *mal du siècle*', concedes that 'nihilistic melancholy' was a 'facet of the transformation of Europe which we call "romanticism".'[15] Nihilism itself was an idea that first appeared in the 1790s; the word was coined by the German Romantic progenitor, Friedrich Jacobi. Melancholy, too, though not a word coined by the Romantics, was, as Victor Hugo emphasizes, a special feature of that sensibility. He speaks of 'a new sentiment, unknown to the ancients and singularly developed in the moderns, a sentiment that is more than seriousness and less than sadness: melancholy'.[16] And yet it was often

[12] Thomas McFarland, *Originality and Imagination* (Baltimore: The Johns Hopkins University Press, 1985), 72.   [13] Praz, 31.
[14] *Œuvres complètes de Gustave Flaubert. Correspondance.* Première série (1830–50)(Paris: Louis Conard, 1910), 44.
[15] Richard Fargher, *Life and Letters in France; The Eighteenth Century* (New York: Charles Scribner's Sons, 1970), 75.
[16] Victor Hugo, *Théâtre complet*, ed. Roland Purnal, J.-J. Thierry, and Josette Mélèze, Bibliothèque de la Pléiade (Paris: Gallimard, 1963–4), i. 414.

more than sadness. Nerval, who saluted the 'black sun of melancholy',[17] committed suicide.

His or the other suicides of the era give us an entry into the innermost essence of Romanticism. As suggested in the previous chapter, all the seemingly heterogeneous manifestations of Romanticism can be derived from a single truth that constitutes the Romantic core. That truth is the diminishment of man's sense of self and its value. The central truth of Romanticism is not joy and fullness of being but what Hegel, in a pregnant phrase, called 'the unhappy consciousness'—'das unglückliche Bewußtsein'.[18] The unhappy consciousness was a consciousness of irreconcilable conflict, was 'the consciousness of self as a divided nature, a doubled and merely contradictory being'.[19] A modern commentator, Judith Shklar, enlarges on the relationship of the phrase to the inner nature of Romanticism:

The aesthetic revolt of romanticism was ... only part of a more general dissatisfaction with the entire age. If we look deeper, beyond even the conscious expressions of romantic thought, we discover a specific consciousness ... described by Hegel as the 'unhappy consciousness'. This is the 'alienated soul' that has lost all faith in the beliefs of the past, having been disillusioned by skepticism, but is unable to find a new home for its spiritual longings in the present or future. Hopelessly tossed back and forth between memory and yearning, it can neither accept the present nor face the new world. . . . It was not only that 'God is dead,' but that culture had perished. . . . The sense of lostness in the 'real' world that marks the unhappy consciousness, and that lies at the root of the romantic revival, is also what gives the movement its continuity.[20]

Another commentator, Eric Newton, uses a different formulation to indicate the same situation:

I am inclined to think that the advent of romantic movements is a by-product of the decay of humanism. . . . This consciousness . . . always results in Man being displaced from his central position as the measure of all things and being involved once more in a struggle . . . which always belittles him.[21]

---

[17] Nerval, i, 29.   [18] Hegel, iii. 163.

[19] Ibid. 'Das unglückliche Bewußtsein aber *findet* sich nur als *begehrend* und *arbeitend*; es ist für es nicht vorhanden, daß, sich so zu finden, die innere Gewißheit seiner selbst zum Grunde liegt und sein Gefühl des Wesens dies Selbstgefühl ist. Indem es sie *für sich selbst* nicht hat, bleibt sein Inneres vielmehr noch die gebrochene Gewißheit seiner selbst; die Bewährung, welche es durch Arbeit und Genuß erhalten würde, ist darum eine ebensolche *gebrochene*; oder es muß sich vielmehr selbst diese Bewährung Vernichten, so daß es in ihr wohl die Bewährung, aber nur die Bewährung desjenigen, was es für sich ist, nämlich seiner Entzweiung findet' (170).

[20] Judith N. Shklar, *After Utopia: The Decline of Political Faith* (Princeton: Princeton University Press, 1969 [1957]), 15–16.

[21] Eric Newton, *The Romantic Rebellion* (New York: Schocken Books, 1964 [1962]), 62.

Only a certain amount of Romantic activity constitutes a direct expression of the 'unhappy consciousness', but it does seem true that all Romantic criteria, if we consider reaction formations as well as direct responses, translate into varying strategies for coping with the single fact of a mounting pressure on the ego. Whether that pressure was psychological, economic, religious, philosophical, sociological, political, whether it came singly or in series, it created emptiness and despair. Nerval committed suicide for religious as well as psychological reasons; Lamb's friend Benjamin Haydon committed suicide ostensibly for economic reasons alone; Chatterton committed suicide for a complex of sociological, psychological, and economic reasons. Others did it or contemplated it for philosophical reasons. 'The authentic philosophical act is suicide,' wrote Novalis; 'this is the real beginning of all philosophy.'[22] A figure of iconic nihilism is the French poet Escousse, who in 1832 committed suicide, along with his friend Le Braz, and left this note:

Escousse has killed himself because he does not feel at home down here, because energy is lacking for every step forward or backward, because the love of glory does not dominate his soul enough, if there is a soul.[23]

Lamb did not commit suicide, though his situation might have indicated such a course.[24] The severest pressure short of suicide, however, which was madness, was endemic, both for Romanticism and for the environs of Lamb's life, whether we think of Cowper and his drowning gulfs in 1800, of Hölderlin and his tower in 1807, or Mary Lamb and her knife in 1796. And it would be difficult to say whether the suicide Kleist (who considered his life 'das allerqualvollste, das je ein Mensch geführt hat'—'the most tormented that ever a man has lived'),[25] was more unhappy than the madman Clare.

Indeed, Mary Lamb's homely proximity to Charles Lamb and his charm symbolizes the truth that madness and suicide lay all around. Lamb's friend Charles Lloyd was quite mad;[26] his friend Coleridge's life was one long neurotic crisis; his friend Godwin, though sane and

[22] Novalis Schriften: Die Werke Friedrich von Hardenbergs, ed. Paul Kluckhohn and Richard Samuels, 2nd ed. (Stuttgart: W. Kohlhammer Verlag, 1960–), ii. 395.
[23] Max Milner, Le Romantisme; I; 1820–1843 (Paris: B. Arthaud, 1973), 199.
[24] For, as Wordsworth says of him, he was beset 'by troubles strange, / Many and strange, that hung about his life' (Wordsworth, Poems, iv. 273).
[25] Heinrich von Kleists Werke, ed. Erich Schmidt (Leipzig and Vienna: Bibliographisches Institut, 1904–06), v. 435.
[26] For an account, at once vivid and sympathetic, of Lloyd and his madness, see De Quincey, Recollections, 313–33.

optimistic, can be seen, as reported by Charles Kegan Paul, giving
heroic arguments against suicide to a young disciple, who nevertheless
went on to do the deed, as did Godwin's own daughter, Fanny. In the
aftermath of Mary's murder of their mother, Lamb wrote of his brother,
who, though twelve years older, was ineffectual as a support, 'Since this
has happened he has been very kind & brotherly; but I fear for his
mind,—he has taken his ease in the world, & is not fit himself to struggle
with difficulties. . . . He can be very good, but I fear for his mind.'[27]

Lamb himself broke down late in 1795, before, not after, the horror of
his sister's deed, and was confined in an asylum for six weeks. He reports
the matter with his customary strategic whimsy:

. . . my life has been somewhat diversified of late. The 6 weeks that finished last
year & began this your very humble servant spent very agreeably in a mad house
at Hoxton—. I am got somewhat rational now, & dont bite any one. But mad I
was & many a vagary my imagination played with me, enough to make a volume if
all told—[28]

We can only guess at the contents of that volume, for Lamb has mounted
all his defences against despair. But madness is a serious business, and
not even Lamb's heroic deployment of whimsy can entirely resist the
onset of darkness. 'In your absence', he later writes to Coleridge,

the tide of melancholy rushd in again, & did its worst Mischief by overwhelming my Reason. I have recoverd. But feel a stupor that makes me indifferent to
the hopes & fears of this life. . . . A correspondence, opening with you has
roused me a little from my lethargy. . . . Indulge me in it. I will not be very
troublesome. at some future time I will amuse you with an account . . . of the
strange turn my phrensy took. . . . Dream not Coleridge, of having tasted all the
grandeur & wildness of Fancy, till you have gone mad. All now seems to me
vapid; comparatively so. Excuse this selfish digression—[29]

But though here the seriousness of being mad almost overwhelms the
defences of whimsy, the last earthwork of politeness still protects the
wounded self: 'Excuse this selfish digression'; 'I will not be very
troublesome.' And a quick return to whimsy is promised: 'at some future
time I will amuse you with an account . . . of the strange turn my phrensy
took.' It was Mary's frenzy, however, that took the next strange turn,
Mary who thenceforth made the repeated trips to the asylum; while her
brother, hanging on by his fingernails over the abyss, and with miles to

[27] Lamb, *Letters*, i. 50. 3 Oct. 1796.   [28] Ibid. 3–4. 27 May 1796.
[29] Ibid. 18–19. 9 June 1796.

go before he slipped, never let go again.[30] 'God bless us all,' he said at the close of a letter, 'and shield us from insanity, which is the sorest malady of all.'[31]

Because of his narrow circumstances of life and experience, and his Sisyphean labours at the East India House, Lamb was not able to avail himself of other Romantic modes of lifting the pressures on the ego. External nature had been a balm and escape for almost all Romantics. 'My imagination', Rousseau had said, 'languishes and dies in a room beneath the rafters of a ceiling'; it 'only thrives in the country and under the trees.'[32] Accordingly, when he quit Paris for his bucolic sojourn at the Hermitage, Rousseau says:

Although for some years I had fairly frequently gone into the country, I had hardly tasted its pleasures. Indeed my trips, generally made in the company of pretentious people and always ruined by a feeling of constraint, had merely whetted my appetite for rural delights; the closer the glimpse I got of them the more I felt the want of them. I was so tired of reception rooms, fountains, shrubberies, and flower-beds . . . I was so weary of pamphlets, clavichords . . . and great dinners, that when I spied a poor simple thorn bush, a hedge, a barn, or a meadow . . . when I heard in the distance the rustic refrain of the goat-women's song, I consigned all rouge, flounces, and perfumes to the devil.[33]

Elsewhere Rousseau says that 'I felt that I was born for retirement and the country; it was impossible for me to live happily anywhere else'.[34]

But Lamb, with his urban obligations, could not look for such escape.[35] To be sure, he celebrated the happiness of life in the city:

I shall be as airy, up 4 pair of stairs, as in the country; & in a garden in the midst of enchanting more than Mahometan paradise London, whose dirtiest drab-frequented alley, and her lowest bowing Tradesman, I would not exchange for Skiddaw, Helvellyn, James, Walter, and the Parson [i.e. in Wordsworth's 'The Brothers'] in the bargain—. O! her Lamps of a night! her rich goldsmiths, print shops, toy shops, mercers, hardwaremen, pastry cooks! . . . These are thy Gods O London—.[36]

---

[30] As Patmore recalled many years later, 'The truth is that, deep and yet gentle as [Lamb's] affections were, his daily life gave token that in their early development they had received a sinister bias which never afterwards quitted them—perchance a blow which struck them from the just centre on which they seemed to have been originally destined . . .' (Patmore, i. 67). [31] Lamb, Letters, i. 109. 15 Apr. 1797.
[32] Rousseau, i. 428. [33] Ibid. 412–13. [34] Ibid. 400.
[35] Lamb already loved Rousseau, however. E.g.: 'I love them [Coleridge's intimate verses] as I love the Confessions of Rousseau, and for the same reason: the same frankness, the same openness of heart, the same disclosure of all the most hidden and delicate affections of the mind . . .' (Lamb, Letters, i. 59. 8 Nov. 1796).
[36] Ibid. i. 277. 27 Feb. 1801.

There can be no doubt that Lamb did love city life; but that he seemed much to prefer it to the nature-enchantments proselytized by Coleridge and Wordsworth must at least take into account the fact that he had no other real choice.[37] It is precisely the truth that Lamb always accepted the yoke of circumstance, no matter how heavy it might have been, with humour and assent instead of with rebellion. As he writes to Wordsworth:

I have passed all my days in London, until I have formed as many and intense local attachments, as any of you Mountaineers can have done with dead nature. The Lighted shops of the Strand and Fleet Street, the innumerable trades, tradesmen and customers, coaches, waggons, play houses, all the bustle and wickedness round about Covent Garden, the very women of the Town, the Watchmen, drunken scenes, rattles;—life awake, if you awake, at all hours of the night, the impossibility of being dull in Fleet Street, the crowds, the very dirt & mud . . . the old Book stalls . . . all these things work themselves into my mind and feed me. . . . The wonder of these sights impells me into night-walks about her crowded streets, and I often shed tears in the motley Strand from fullness of joy at so much Life—. All these emotions must be strange to you. So are your rural emotions to me.—But consider, what must I have been doing all my life, not to have lent great portions of my heart with usury to such scenes?[38]

Coleridge, in 'This Lime-Tree Bower my Prison', seems to think that Lamb actually pined for the country;[39] and though Coleridge may to some extent have been projecting his own sentiments onto his friend, as he was quite capable of doing, we may at least listen to his voice:

> Yes! they wonder on
> In gladness all; but thou, methinks, most glad,
> My gentle-hearted Charles! for thou hast
>   pined
> And hunger'd after Nature, many a year,
> In the great City pent, winning thy way
> With sad yet patient soul, through evil and
>   pain
> And strange calamity![40]

---

[37] Thus Wordsworth cannily observes: 'Thou wert a scorner of the fields, my Friend, / But more in show than truth . . .' (Wordsworth, *Poems*, iv. 274.)

[38] Lamb, *Letters*, i. 267. 30 Jan. 1801.

[39] Certainly Lamb did show the most intense enthusiasm for possible proximity to Coleridge. 'O. Col: would to God you were in London with us, or we two at Stowey with you all—' (Lamb, *Letters*, i. 93. 16 Jan. 1797). Perhaps even more intensely: 'I discern a possibility of my paying you a visit *next week*. May I, can I, shall I come so soon? Have you *room* for me, *leisure* for me . . . ?' (i. 113. 24 June 1797).

[40] Coleridge, *Poems*, i. 179.

When Coleridge left town in 1796, Lamb felt bereft. 'You came to Town', he writes, '& I saw you at a time when your heart was yet bleeding with recent wounds. Like yourself, I was sore galled with disappointed Hope. . . . When you left London I felt a dismal void in my heart, I found myself cut off at one & the same time from two most dear to me.'[41] The other person Lamb refers to is Ann Simmons. But it was Coleridge who seems to have figured most in the depression. Lamb's brother claimed that Coleridge was really responsible for Lamb's breakdown,[42] and Lamb himself noted that it was 'in your absence' that 'the tide of melancholy rushed in again, & did its worst Mischief by overwhelming my Reason'.[43]

Be that as it may, to be around Coleridge Lamb had to be in the country, and so it may well be that from Coleridge's perspective, Lamb's gladness did seem to result from being in nature after being 'pent' in the great City.[44] That, indeed, was Coleridge's own situation with respect to Wordsworth, 'his God Wordsworth' as Lamb said, perhaps not entirely without jealousy.[45] We glimpse the unrealized possibilities of Lamb's Romantic love of nature in his reaction to a visit to the Lake District. 'My final resolve was a tour to the Lakes', he writes to Manning in September 1802:

I set out with Mary to Keswick, without giving Coleridge any notice . . . ; he received us with all the hospitality in the world, and gave up his time to shew us all the wonders of the country. He dwells upon a small hill by the side of Keswick, in a comfortable house, quite enveloped on all sides by a net of mountains: great floundering bears & monsters they seem'd, all couchant & asleep. We got in in the evening, travelling in a Post-Chaise from Penrith, in the midst of a gorgeous sun shine, which transmuted all the mountains into colours. . . . We thought we had got into Fairy Land. . . . We entered Coleridge's comfortable study just in the dusk, when the mountains were all dark with clouds upon their heads. Such an impression I never received from objects of sight before, nor do I suppose that I can ever again. Glorious

---

[41] Lamb, *Letters*, i. 18. 9 June 1796.

[42] '. . . much as he dwelt upon your conversation while you were among us, and delighted to be with you, it has been his fashion ever since to depreciate and cry you down,—you were the cause of my madness—you and your damned foolish sensibility and melancholy—and he lamented with a true brotherly feeling that we ever met . . .' (Lamb, *Letters*, i. 78. 10 Dec. 1796).   [43] See above, Chap. 2, n. 29.

[44] For instance, using the very word 'pent' (which seems to have had a special currency in the conversations of Coleridge and Wordsworth), Lamb writes to Manning on 29 July 1800: 'I need not describe the expectations which such an one as myself, pent up all my life in a dirty city, have formed of a tour to the *Lakes*. Consider, Grassmere! Ambleside! Wordsworth! Coleridge!' (Lamb, *Letters*, i. 247).   [45] Ibid. 191. 5 Apr. 1800.

creatures, fine old fellows, Skiddaw, &c. . . . Coleridge had got a blazing fire in his study, which is a large antique ill-shaped room, with an old-fashioned organ, never play'd upon, big enough for a church, Shelves of scattered folios, an Eolian Harp, & an old sofa, half-bed &c. And all looking out upon the last fading view of Skiddaw & his broad-breasted brethren: What a night![46]

It seems clear that Coleridge played an important part in Lamb's being impressed by the natural scene, but it also seems clear that he was nonetheless impressed by it:

. . . . we have seen Keswick, Grasmere, Ambleside, Ulswater (where the Clarksons live) and a place at the other end of Ulswater, I forget the name, to which we travelled on a very sultry day over the middle of Helvellyn. We have clambered up to the top of Skiddaw, & I have waded up the bed of Lodore. In fine, I have satisfied myself, that there is such a thing as that, which tourists call *romantic*, which I very much suspected before. . . .[47]

His three-week sojourn over, Lamb left for London, accepting as always the yoke of the East India House; but we are surely justified in hearing a tone of regret that the Romantic option of escape into nature was never really open for him:

Mary was excessively tired, when she got about half way up Skiddaw, but we came to a cold rill (than which nothing can be imagined more cold, running over cold stones) & with the reinforcement of a draught of cold water, she surmounted it most manfully. O its fine black head & the bleak air a top of it, with a prospect of mountains all about & about, making you giddy, & then Scotland afar off & the border countries so famous in song & ballad—. It was a day that will stand out, like a mountain, I am sure, in my life.—But I am returned (I have now been come home near 3 weeks (I was a month out) & you cannot conceive the degradation I felt at first, from being accustommed to wander free as air among mountains, & bathe in rivers without being controuled by any one, to come home & *work*: I felt very *little*. I had been dreaming I was a very great man. But that is going off, & I find I shall conform in time to that state of Life, to which it has pleased God to call me. Besides, after all, Fleet Street & the Strand are better places to live in for good & all than among Skiddaw: Still, I turn back to those great places, where I wandered about, participating in their greatness. After all I could not *live* in Skiddaw: I could spend a year, two, three years, among them, but I must have a prospect of seeing Fleet Street at the End of that time: or I should mope & pine away, I know. Still Skiddaw is a fine Creature.[48]

The Sisyphean stone of Lamb's duties at the East India House, and the weight of family responsibility ('I had the whole weight of the family thrown on me', he once noted) also blocked out other Romantic modes

[46] Ibid. ii. 68–9.   [47] Ibid. 69.   [48] Ibid. 69–70.

of lifting the pressures on the ego.[49] Lamb could not indulge in drugs, as his non-working friend Coleridge did, nor could be seek the artificial paradises of De Quincey and Baudelaire. His job at the East India House could not tolerate such inattention. As Winifred Courtney notes, 'Fat ledgers contained what Lamb called his "true works"—the endless jottings and tottings required by the vast commercial establishment the East India Company then was.'[50]

Likewise, the dominating Romantic motif of medievalism—the 'fantastic mania for the medieval'[51] as Uhland called it—was not much of a possibility for him. Ann Radcliffe could have her various haunted castles, Victor Hugo his *Notre-Dame de Paris*, even Wordsworth his 'Horn of Egremont Castle'; but Lamb could not range so widely in dream or reverie. The same held true for indulgence in the other Romantic imaginary land of escape, the Orient (Southey wallowed in a kind of mélange of medievalism and orientalism in his *Curse of Kehama*). Nor could he much avail himself of the erotic freedom prescribed by Friedrich Schlegel's *Lucinde* and actually lived by Byron and even Shelley. Nor could he indulge in Romantic wanderlust, the questing voyages that were more escapes than discoveries. Chateaubriand travelled memorably to America; Chateaubriand travelled to the Orient too. But Chateaubriand was a nobleman, as was Byron, whose life and works were dominated by Romantic wanderlust; and both Byron and the scion of wealth, Shelley, were financially able to move to the heterocosmic realm of Italy.

None of this was available to Lamb. He had to exist within a narrow

[49] 'Sisyphean' is a word that rises naturally to describe Lamb's situation at the East India House. Thus De Quincey: 'Lamb was summoned, it is true, through the larger and more genial section of his life, to the drudgery of a copying clerk.... Such a labour of Sisyphus,—the rolling up a ponderous stone to the summit of a hill in that it might roll back again ... seems a bad employment for a man of genius in his meridian energies' (*De Quincey*, v. 226–7). Lamb agreed. 'I have left the d——d India House for Ever! Give me great joy.'—that is his one-line letter to Crabb Robinson in 1825 (Lucas, ii. 465. 29 Mar. 1825). To Wordsworth the next week he says: 'Here I am after 33 years of slavery, sitting in my own room at 11 o'Clock this finest of April mornings a freed man, with £441 a year for the remainder of my life' (Lucas, ii. 466. 6 Apr. 1825).

[50] Winifred F. Courtney, *Young Charles Lamb, 1775–1802* (London and Basingstoke: The Macmillan Press Ltd., 1982), 101.

[51] 'Die Romantik ist nicht bloß ein phantastischer Wahn des Mittelalters; sie ist hohe, ewige Poesie, die im Bilde darstellt, was Worte dürftig oder nimmer aussprechen, sie ist das Buch seltsamer Zauberbilder, die uns in Verkehr erhalten mit der dunkeln Geisterwelt; sie ist der schimmernde Regenbogen, die Brücke der Götter, worauf, nach der Edda, sie zu den Sterblichen herab und die Auserwählten zu ihnen emporsteigen' (*Uhland*, ii. 350–1). Uhland himself was not only a significant Romantic poet but became a major professional scholar of the medieval period as well.

compass, discharging the obligations accepted by his deeply honourable nature, holding off the terrors of existence and maintaining his supporting friendships by a complex and politic system of whimsy and charm. Perhaps his sense of being cheated out of the pleasures of eroticism and travel lies at the root of his uncharacteristic severity toward Byron and Shelley. He wrote,

I can no more understand Shelley than you can. For his theories and nostrums they are oracular enough, but I either comprehend 'em not, or there is miching malice and mischief in 'em. But for the most part ringing with their own emptiness. Hazlitt said well of 'em—Many are wiser and better for reading Shakespeare, but nobody was ever wiser or better for reading Shelley.[52]

Browning's awe at the man who once saw Shelley plain might have been tempered by consulting Lamb: 'Shelly I saw once. His voice was the most obnoxious squeak I ever was tormented with . . .'[53] Byron was judged with equal harshness: 'I have a thorough aversion to his character,' said Lamb, 'and a very moderate admiration of his genius—he is great in so little a way.'[54] On Byron's death, Lamb could not produce the expected bromides:

He was to me offensive, and I never can make out his great *power*, which his admirers talk of. Why, a line of Wordsworth's is a lever to lift the immortal spirit! Byron can only move the Spleen. He was at best a Satyrist,—in any other way he was mean enough. I dare say I do him injustice; but I cannot love him, nor squeeze a tear to his memory.[55]

However harsh he could be towards rivals such as Byron and Shelley, who had freedoms he could only dream of, Lamb was enormously involved with and respectful of Coleridge and Wordsworth. Both were essential to his psychic defences. With no support from an ineffectual father, and no support from an ineffectual brother, Lamb in his struggle for survival needed substitutes for both, and hence it was that he treated Coleridge and Wordsworth with such politic deference, expending mountainous charm in his attempt to avoid confrontation. As was suggested by quotations above, Coleridge was undoubtedly, next to Mary, and in all positive senses more than Mary, the most important figure in his life, the closest thing to a caring father and brother that Lamb ever found; for the dependable Manning seems clearly a substi-

---

[52] Lucas, ii. 436–7.   [53] Ibid. 338.   [54] Ibid. 279.
[55] Ibid. 426.

tute for the absent and erratic Coleridge.[56] The fact that Coleridge's own temperament made him not a very sound rock upon which to build was experienced by Lamb but not wholly admitted by him. After Coleridge's death in 1834 and shortly before his own, Lamb recalled his friend in terms of overwhelming idealism and need:

I feel how great a part he was of me. His great and dear spirit haunts me. I cannot think a thought, I cannot make a criticism on men or books, without an ineffectual turning and reference to him. He was the proof and touchstone of all my cogitations. . . . He was my fifty years old friend without a dissension. Never saw I his likeness, nor probably the world can see again.[57]

A fifty years friend, yes, but without dissension, no. Around the turn of the century, Lamb had had serious dissension with Coleridge, and for a time the friendship was in virtual abeyance. Lamb cites a report that 'Sam. Taylor Coleridge appears to him as much as ever under the influence of a cold vanity.'[58] This in September 1801. In December

---

[56] Lamb never lost the intensity of his need for Coleridge. It was rather Coleridge's elusiveness that caused the seeming diminution in the friendship. As Lamb writes in April, 1797: 'Your last letter was dated the 10th February; in it you promised to write again the next day. At least I did not expect so long, so unfriendlike, a silence' (Lamb, *Letters*, i. 105). On June 12: 'I stared with wild wonderment to see thy well-known hand again. It revived many a pleasing recollection of an epistolary intercourse of late strangely suspended, once the pride of my life' (i. 110). Lamb gradually adjusted to the one-sidedness of the relationship. 'Where is Coleridge?' he asks Wordsworth on 28 December 1814 (ii. 125). On 5 May 1815 he says to Southey: 'Of Coleridge I hear nothing, nor of the Morgans. I hope to have him like a reappearing star standing up before me some time when least expected in London' (iii. 156). By now, instead of writing to Coleridge himself, he had long since learned to write to Morgan: 'There—do'nt read any further, because the Letter is not intended for you but for Coleridge, who perhaps might not have opened it directed to him suo nomine' (iii. 74. 8 Mar. 1811). To Wordsworth in 1816 Lamb writes: 'I have seen Colerge. but once this 3 or 4 months, he is an odd person, when he first comes to town he is quite hot upon visiting, and then he turns off & absolutely never comes at all, but seems to forget there are any such people in the world' (iii. 225. 23 Sept. 1816). To Southey in 1818: 'I do not see S. T. C. so often as I could wish. He never comes to me; and though his host and hostess [the Gillmans] are very friendly, it puts me out of my way to go see one person at another person's house' (Lucas, ii. 234. 26 Oct. 1818). The situation was summed up by Mary Lamb in a letter of 10 December 1808: 'Do not imagine that I am now *complaining* to you of Coleridge, perhaps we are both in fault. We expect *too much*, and he gives *too little*. . . . [H]e will some day or other come in with the same old face, and receive (after a few spiteful words from me) the same warm welcome as ever' (Lamb, *Letters*, ii. 289). Coleridge, for his part, at one point suggested that he visited Lamb less because Hazlitt was there: 'I could not speak to C. Lamb or you & Mary—because that unhappy man Hazlitt (to the credit indeed of Charles & Mary Lamb's kindness of Heart—but why need I say that?) is always there—' (Coleridge, *Letters*, iv. 798. To J. J. Morgan, 7 Jan. 1818).   [57] Lucas, i. 351–2.
[58] Lamb, *Letters*, ii. 25. Sept. 1801.

1800 he writes to Manning that 'in Coleridge's letters you will find a
good deal of amusement, to see genuine Talent struggling against a
pompous display of it',[59] and in another statement to Manning of that
same year, he said that 'I cannot but smile at Lloyd's beginning to find
out, that Col[eridge] can tell lyes.'[60] To Coleridge himself, in June
1798, Lamb writes some '*Theses Quaedam Theologicae*' which come close
to an open break. Characteristically, however, Lamb's charges are
oblique and couched in whimsy, however much of a sting they possess.
The first thesis is:

> Whether God loves a lying Angel better than an true Man?

the second:

> Whether the Archangel Uriel *could* affirm an untruth. & if he *could* whether he
> *would*?

and so on down to the eighth and last:

> Whether an immortal & amenable soul may not come to be damned at last, & the
> man never suspect it beforehand?

This, even beneath its disguises, is rather strong stuff, and Lamb
accordingly appends an especially affectionate and whimsical letter that
emphasizes the word friend:

> Learned Sir, my Friend, Presuming on our long habits of friendship . . . I now
> submit to your enquiries the above Theological Propositions, to be by you
> defended, or oppugned, or both, in the Schools of Germany, whither I am told
> you are departing, to the utter dissatisfaction of your native Devonshire, & regret
> of universal England . . .

and so forth. The letter is signed with elaborate and politic deference: 'I
remain / Your friend and docile Pupil to instruct / Charles Lamb.'[61]
    The same deference was extended to Wordsworth and Coleridge as a
pair as was extended to Coleridge alone. A single example suffices.
When Lamb ventured to omit total and effusive praise of all aspects of
the *Lyrical Ballads*, Wordsworth was not pleased, and Coleridge, ever

---

[59] Ibid. i. 261. 19 Dec. 1800.   [60] Ibid. 83. 8 Feb. 1800.
[61] Ibid. 128–9. May–June 1798. Lamb also sent the 'Theses' to Southey, with the
perhaps somewhat sheepish observation that 'Samuel Taylor hath not deign'd an
answer—was it impertinent in me to avail myself of that offer'd source of knowledge?'
(i. 132. 28 July 1798). Lamb later came to feel that it was the irresponsible gossip of
Charles Lloyd that had caused the rift with Coleridge.

Wordsworth's champion, rebuked his disciple. Lamb describes the situation with his inimitable whimsy:

I had need be cautious henceforward what opinion I give of the Lyrical Balads.—All the north of England are in a turmoil. Cumberland and Westmorland have already declared a state of war.—I lately received from Wordsw[orth] a copy of the second volume, accompanied by an acknowledgment of having received from me many months since a copy of a certain Tragedy, with excuses for not having made any acknowledgment sooner, it being owing to an 'almost insurmountable aversion from Letter writing.'—This letter I answered in due form and time, and enumerated several of the passages which had most affected me, adding, unfortunately, that no single piece had moved me so forcibly as the Ancient Marinere, the Mad Mother, or the Lines at Tintern Abbey. The Poet did not sleep a moment. I received almost instantaneously a long letter of four sweating pages from my reluctant Letterwriter, the purport of which was, that he was sorry his 2d vol. had not given me more pleasure (Devil a hint did I give that it had *not pleased me*) and was 'compelled to wish that my range of Sensibility was more extended, being obliged to believe that I should receive large influxes of happiness & happy Thoughts' (I suppose from the L.B.—) With a deal of stuff about a certain 'Union of Tenderness & Imagination, which in the sense he used Imag. was not the characteristic of Shakesp. but which Milton possessed in a degree far exeeding other Poets. . . .'

After further comment, Lamb says:

After one has been reading Shaks. twenty of the best years of one's life, to have a fellow start up, and prate about some unknown quality, which Shakspere possess'd in a degree inferior to Milton and somebody else!!—This was not to be *all* my castigation.—Coleridge, who had not written to me some months before, starts up from his bed of sickness, to reprove me for my hardy presumption: four long pages, equally sweaty, and more tedious, came from him: assuring me, that, when the works of a man of true Genius, such as W. undoubtedly was, do not please me at first sight, I should suspect the fault to lie 'in me & not in them'—&c. &c. &c. &c.— —What am I to do with such people?—I certainly shall write them a very merry Letter.— —[62].

The proposal for 'a very merry Letter' is quintessential Lamb, a microcosmic example of his tactical use of whimsy to avoid confrontation and loss of support.

Despite his great care in avoiding real as opposed to whimsical confrontation with Coleridge and Wordsworth, however, Lamb was very much his own man in critical opinions, as we can infer from his

[62] Lamb, *Letters*, i. 272–73. 15 Feb. 1801.

rebuke of Wordsworth's lack of generosity to the *Ancient Mariner*.[63] He deferred neither to Coleridge nor to Hazlitt in Shakespearean judgements, and he probably knew more about Elizabethan drama than did either of those eminent critics.[64] Again, we may consider De Quincey's report of Lamb's defence of Hazlitt, which seems so just to us today, against both De Quincey's opinion and Coleridge's claims. The anecdote, though idiosyncratic in its recourse to whimsy, also displays the strength and critical discernment of Lamb:

In answer to what I considered Lamb's extravagant estimate of Hazlitt [recalls De Quincey], I had said that the misanthropy which gives so unpleasant a tone to that writer's works was, of itself, sufficient to disgust a reader whose feelings do not happen to flow in that channel; that it was, moreover, a crude misanthropy, not resting upon any consistent basis . . . but simply the peevishness of a disappointed man. . . . Lamb paused a little; but at length said that it was for the intellectual Hazlitt, not the moral Hazlitt, that he professed so much admiration. . . . But, unfortunately, Lamb chose to insinuate . . . that Hazlitt was another Coleridge. . . . This I could not stand. I, whose studies had been chiefly in the field of philosophy, could judge of *that*, if I could judge of anything; and certainly I felt entitled to say that anything which Hazlitt might have attempted in philosophy . . . supposing even that these were not derived entirely from Coleridge . . . could, at the best, be received only as evidences of ingenuity . . . but, for any systematic education or regular course of reading in philosophy, these little works are satisfactory proofs that Hazlitt had them not. . . . Something of this I said. . . . Lamb felt, or counterfeited, a warmth for the moment looked like anger. 'I know not', he said, 'where you have been so lucky as to find finer thinkers than Hazlitt; for my part, I know of none such. You live, I think, or have lived, in Grasmere. Well, I was once there. I was at Keswick, and all over that wild country; yet none such could I find there. But, stay, there are the caves in your neighbourhood, as well as the lakes; these we did not visit. No, Mary,' turning to his sister, 'you know we didn't visit the caves. So, perhaps, these great men live there. Oh! yes, doubtless, they live in the caves of

---

[63] 'I was never so affected with any human Tale. After first reading it, I was totally possessed with it for many days. . . . I totally differ from your idea that the Marinere should have had a character and profession . . . the Ancient Marinere undergoes such Trials, as overwhelm and bury all individuality or memory of what he was.—Like the state of a man in a Bad dream, one terrible peculiarity of which is, that all consciousness of personality is gone.—Your other observation is I think as well a little unfounded. . . . You will excuse my remarks, because I am hurt and vexed that you should think it necessary, with a prose apology, to open the eyes of dead men that cannot see—' (Lamb, *Letters*, i. 266. 30 Jan. 1801).

[64] Cf. Lamb in 1817: 'He [Coleridge] projects a new course, not of physic, nor of metaphysic, nor a new course of life, but a new course of lectures on Shakespear and Poetry. There is no man better qualified (always excepting number one)' (Lucas, ii. 220. 10 Dec. 1817).

Westmoreland. But you must allow for us poor Londoners. Hazlitt serves for *our* purposes. And in this poor, little inconsiderable place of London, he is one of our very prime thinkers. But certainly I ought to have made an exception in behalf of the philosophers in the caves.' And thus he ran on, until it was difficult to know whether to understand him in jest or earnest.[65]

Despite the oblique criticisms of Coleridge in this inimitably Lambian statement, Coleridge, it must be reiterated, was by far the most important intellectual influence, by far the most important friend, who ever entered Lamb's life. 'I have never met with any one,' wrote Lamb to Coleridge in 1796, 'never shall meet with any one, who could or can compensate me for the top of your Society.'[66] Even during the time of their estrangement, Lamb could say:

I am living in a continuous feast [he is writing in March 1800]. Coleridge has been with me now for nigh three weeks, and the more I see of him in the quotidian undress and relaxation of his mind, the more cause I see to love him and believe him a *very good man*, and all those foolish impressions to the contrary fly off like morning slumbers.[67]

It is astonishing to see from this how easily and absolutely Coleridge was able to re-establish his spell over Lamb. In truth, throughout his life Coleridge was for Lamb what earth was for Antaeus, the vivifying, sustaining, and renewing reality; and we can never understand Lamb or his struggle if we in any way fail to recognize the extraordinary depth, constancy, and intensity of his feelings for his friend. 'God bless you,' he writes to Coleridge, 'continue to be my correspondent, & I will strive to fancy that this world is *not* "all barrenness"!'[68] 'Coleridge,' he says again, 'you know not my supreme happiness at having one on earth (though counties separate us) whom I can call friend.'[69] 'Now do write again,' he says again, 'you cannot believe how I long and love always to hear about you.'[70] 'What I have owed to thee', he says yet again, 'my heart can ne'er forget.'[71]

The depth of Lamb's extraordinary commitment to Coleridge must be emphasized, for it provides access to an understanding of the most

[65] *De Quincey*, iii. 82–3.   [66] Lamb, *Letters*, i. 65–6. 1 Dec. 1796.
[67] Ibid. 189. 17 Mar. 1800.
[68] Ibid. 75. 9 Dec. 1796. Again: I thank you . . . from my heart,—& feel myself not quite *alone* in the earth—' (73. 9 Dec. 1796).
[69] Ibid. 32. 14 June 1796.
[70] Ibid. 112. 12 June 1797. Again: 'pray, pray, write to me: if you knew with what anxiety of joy I open such a long packet as you last sent me, you would not grudge giving a few minutes now & then to this intercourse (the *only* intercourse, I fear we two shall ever have).' (67. 1 Dec. 1796).   [71] Ibid. 113. 24 June 1797.

complex ramifications of his politics of survival. Coleridge was not only
brother and father for Lamb (Lamb once said how 'proud' he was to be
'esteemed worthy of the place of friend-confessor, brother-confessor, to
a man like Coleridge');[72] he was, in addition, an intellectual *alter ego*. We
have all, no doubt, looked through opera glasses and seen things made
large; no doubt we have also turned the glasses around and looked
through the other way. Suddenly everything is smaller than life. But
without an instrument that makes everything large we cannot see
everything small. Such was the crucial role of Coleridge in Lamb's
psychic economy. Coleridge was large, Lamb was small. The instrument was their relationship.[73] 'You are very good', Lamb wrote to
Coleridge at one point, 'to submit to be pleased with reading my
nothings.'[74]

    When Lamb looked through the glasses what he saw large was not the
aspiration of Charles Lamb but the aspiration of Coleridge. When he
looked the other way what he saw was another persona, that of Elia.
Without Coleridge, in brief, there would have been no *Essays of Elia*.
Their form and substance were conceived as residue; they were what the
dazzling Coleridge did not pre-empt, for as Lamb wryly noted, though
occasional communion with 'a person of very superior capacity to my
own' had 'constituted the fortune and felicity of my life', the 'habit of too
constant intercourse with spirits above you, instead of raising you, keeps
you down. Too frequent doses of original thinking from others, restrain
what lesser portion of that faculty you may possess on your own.'[75]

    For instance, as I have noted elsewhere, Lamb laid no claim to the
normative Romantic concern with dream and reverie, and in giving up
such involvement he identified the normative state as belonging to
Coleridge:

For the credit of my imagination, I am almost ashamed to say how tame and
prosaic my dreams are grown. They are never romantic. . . . The poverty of my

---

[72] Ibid. 59. 8 Nov. 1796.
[73] 'I love to write to you. I take a pride in it—. It makes me think less meanly of myself'
(Lamb, *Letters*, i. 89. 8 Jan. 1797). 'I can scarce bring myself to believe, that I am admitted
to a familiar correspondence, and all the licence of friendship, with a man who writes blank
verse like Milton' (103. 13 Feb. 1797).   [74] Lamb, *Letters*, i. 104. 13 Feb. 1797.
[75] *Lamb*, ii. 53. Again, to Wordsworth: 'Coleridge is absent but 4 miles, & the
neighbourhood of such a man is as exciting as the presence of 50 ordinary Persons. Tis
enough to be within the whiff & wind of *his* genius, for us not to possess our souls in
quiet.—If I lived with him or the *Author of the Excursion*, I should in a very little time lose
my own identity, & be dragged along in the current of other peoples thoughts, hampered in
a net' (Lamb, *Letters*, iii. 215. 26 Apr. 1816).

dreams mortifies me. There is Coleridge, at his will can conjure up icy domes, and pleasure-houses for Kubla Khan, and Abyssinian maids, and songs of Abora . . . when I cannot muster a fiddle.[76]

Yet Lamb, his self-deprecation notwithstanding, produced—in prose—the poignant longing of 'Dream Children: A Reverie'. The fact that the essay was in prose was also the little-ended Elia transformation of the large-ended poetic or Coleridgean vision. Lamb had in fact started out with aspirations towards poetry. 'My Sonnets', he writes to Coleridge in May of 1796, 'I have extended to the number of nine since I saw you';[77] and later he says, 'I am beginning a poem in blank verse, which if I finish I publish.'[78] By September of that year, however, his mood has changed: '[M]ention nothing of poetry. I have destroyed every vestige of past vanities of that kind.'[79] The more he retreated into prose, however—'I love you in all the naked honesty of prose', he wrote to Coleridge—the more his *alter ego* rose in his poetic esteem.[80] Of Coleridge's *Religious Musings* he says: 'I was reading your Religious Musings the other day, & sincerely I think it the noblest poem in the language, next after the Paradise lost, & even that was not made the vehicle of such grand truths.'[81] Significantly, he also said of the *Religious Musings*, 'when I read them, I think how poor, how unelevated, unoriginal, my blank verse is'.[82]

The giving-up of aspiration in poetry was co-ordinate with another of Lamb's renunciations of largeness in life. Speaking to Coleridge of 'my sonnets', he says, 'I blush that my mind can consider them as things of any worth. . . . [D]o not entitle any of my *things* Love Sonnets, as I told you to call 'em, 'twill only make me look little in my own eyes; for it is a passion of which I retain nothing.'[83]

---

[76] *Lamb*, ii. 69. Cf. Hazlitt: 'Coleridge used to laugh at me for my want of the faculty of dreaming; and once, on my saying that I did not like the preternatural stories in the Arabian Nights . . . he said, "That must be because you never dream. There is a class of poetry built on this foundation, which is surely no inconsiderable part of our nature, since we are asleep and building up imaginations of this sort half our time." I had nothing to say against it; it was one of his conjectural subtleties, in which he excels all the persons I ever knew; . . . . Yet I dream sometimes; I dream of the Louvre' (Hazlitt, xii. 23–4). But contrast De Quincey: 'In dreams, perhaps under some secret conflict of the midnight sleeper, lighted up to the consciousness at the time, but darkened to the memory as soon as all is finished, each several child of our mysterious race completes for himself the treason of the aboriginal fall' (*De Quincey*, xiii. 304). [77] Lamb, *Letters*, i. 4. 27 May 1796.
[78] Ibid. [79] Ibid. 45. 27 Sept. 1796. [80] Ibid. 92. 16 Jan. 1797.
[81] Ibid. 95. 5 Feb. 1797.
[82] Ibid. 66. 1 Dec. 1796. Again: 'You have put me out of conceit with my blank verse by your Religious Musings' (22. 10 June 1796). [83] Ibid. 60. 28 Oct. 1796.

As Lamb retreated into smallness and prose, he projected for his *alter ego* Coleridge the ultimate largeness of poetry. He addresses his friend in January 1797,

Coleridge, I want you to write an Epic poem. Nothing short of it can satisfy the vast capacity of true poetic genius. Having one great End to direct all your poetical faculties to, & on which to lay out your hopes, your ambition, will shew you to what you are equal. By the sacred energies of Milton, by the dainty sweet and soothing phantasies of hony-tongued Spencer, I adjure you to attempt the Epic.[84]

Coleridge attempted, and, characteristically for him and for the rup-tured nature of Romanticism, failed. Lamb, in prose, at the small end of the vision, attempted and in a sense succeeded. For the twenty-eight prose essays of Elia are as surely the record of Lamb's psychic odyssey as are the twenty-four books of Homer's epic a record of Odysseus' journey. To be sure, the inner spirit of Charles Lamb is deeply fortified within the *Essays of Elia*, which are as complicated as an interlocking series of earthworks and star fortifications by Vauban. The figure on the inner parapet, though dressed as Lamb, is not Lamb but Elia. Where Lamb had accepted diminution as necessary to his survival as East India accountant and Mary-supporter ('I felt very *little*', he recalled after returning to his duties from his Keswick vacation, but 'I shall conform in time to that state of Life to which it has pleased God to call me'),[85] he makes Elia even smaller. The name Elia, in fact, is simply Lamb's initial, L, which he used frequently, with a diminutive ending that indicates heterogeneous fragmentation, as in juvenilia or trivia.

Of course earlier essayists had also availed themselves of narrative personae, but Sir Roger de Coverly and Isaac Bickerstaff are not at all like Elia. As a commentator has noted:

Elia . . . is notable for his professed limitations of character and knowledge. He repeatedly refers to his unimportance. He professes to know little about history and chronology. Of geography he has less knowledge than a very young schoolboy. 'In everything that relates to science, I am a whole Encyclopedia behind the rest of the world', he admits. He depreciates his own activities and defers quite often to the opinions of another. . . . He appears as an ineffectual presence in the daily affairs of man.[86]

---

[84] Ibid. 87. 8 Jan. 1797.   [85] Ibid. ii. 70. 24 Sept. 1802.
[86] Robert Frank, *Don't Call me Gentle Charles: An Essay on Lamb's 'Essays of Elia'* (Corvallis: Oregon State University Press, 1976), 20.

In the essays themselves Lamb says that 'no one whose mind is introspective—and mine is painfully so—can have a less respect for his present identity, than I have for the man Elia'.[87] He warns again, 'let no one receive the narratives of Elia for true records! They are, in truth, but shadows of fact—verisimilitudes, not verities.'[88]

But I suggest that in the intertext of the essayistic verisimilitudes we can repeatedly discern the verities of Lamb's beleaguered existence.[89] The essays themselves, to change the metaphor, are the chambers of an Egyptian pyramid designed to delude the curious into thinking the tomb is empty; and the false guide, Elia, continually assures us, whimsically, that there are no bodies here. Nevertheless, many of the rooms do contain bodies, not publicly exhibited in stately crypts, but concealed under the floor. 'Not that I affect ignorance', says Elia disarmingly, 'but my head has not many mansions, nor spacious; and I have been obliged to fill it with such cabinet curiosities as it can hold without aching.'[90] Yet the head, as we know, was the same head referred to in our representative anecdote: 'I am completely shipwreck'd—My head is quite bad. . . I almost wish Mary were dead.'[91] 'I must be serious, circumspect, & deeply religious thro' life,' he had early on decided, '& by such means may *both* of us escape madness in future if it so please the Almighty—.'[92] Underneath their whimsy, the *Essays of Elia* are deeply serious, and heroically circumspect.

If we inspect their cabinet curiosities in this light, therefore, we see that each has a subtext of desperation. I shall do no more than sketch and suggest, and that only briefly. But if we consider the first essay, 'The South-Sea House', we see under its verisimilitude of charm and whimsy the verity of the Tartarus in which Lamb laboured for thirty-three years.[93] Elia attempts to 'divert' us—divert is his word—'with some half-forgotten humours of some old clerks defunct, in an old house of business, long since gone to decay.'[94] In the second essay, 'Oxford in the Vacation', we hear, underneath the whimsical verisimilitude, the blight-

---

[87] *Lamb*, ii. 28.   [88] Ibid. 90.

[89] 'I retire, impenetrable to ridicule, under the phantom cloud of Elia' (*Lamb*, ii. 29). As De Quincey observed, 'The mercurialities of Lamb were infinite, and always uttered in a spirit of absolute recklessness for the quality or the prosperity of a sally. It seemed to liberate his spirits from some burthen of blackest melancholy which oppressed it, when he had thrown off a jest' (*De Quincey*, v. 253).   [90] *Lamb*, ii. 49.

[91] Lamb, *Letters*, i. 203. 12 May 1800.   [92] Ibid. 51. 3 Oct. 1796.

[93] 'I hate all such people—Accountants, Deputy Accountants. The dear abstract notion of the East India Company, as long as she is unseen, is pretty, rather Poetical; but as SHE makes herself manifest by the persons of such Beasts, I loathe and detest her as the Scarlet what-do-you-call-her of Babylon' (Lucas, ii. 228. 18 Feb. 1818).   [94] *Lamb*, ii. 7.

ing verity of Lamb's deprivation of the chance of a university education
—and here the rage is near the surface. 'To such a one as myself,' he
lightly says, 'who has been defrauded in his young years of the sweet
food of academic institution, nowhere is so pleasant, to while away a few
idle weeks at, as one or other of the Universities.'[95]

The third essay, 'Christ's Hospital Five and Thirty Years Ago', sets
up in the verity beneath its simular charm the huge-dimensioned figure
of Coleridge on whom Lamb all his life projected his defrauded
intellectual hopes: 'Come back into memory, like as thou wert in the
day-spring of thy fancies ... Samuel Taylor Coleridge—Logician,
Metaphysician, Bard!'[96]

This celebrated essay, indeed, shows the need for such a heroic *alter
ego* by recalling the utter abandonment which a lonely and frightened
boy felt: 'I was a poor friendless boy. My parents, and those who should
care for me, were far away. . . . O the cruelty of separating a poor lad
from his early homestead'.[97] To be sure, the friendless West-Country
boy cast alone into London represented Coleridge even more than
Lamb; but Lamb merges with Coleridge here, entering into the
splendour and the constriction of a career that was more extreme than
his own at both poles.

The fourth essay, 'The Two Races of Men', speaks with whimsical
jollity of 'two distinct races, *the men who borrow*, and *the men who lend*.'[98]
Its darker verity is the distinction between those who take from life
—erotically and selfishly—such as Byron and Shelley, and those from
whom life takes, those who labour and are heavy-laden, like Lamb. The
whimsical noting of how Coleridge borrowed Lamb's books has its rage
near the surface, and the books borrowed stand symbolically for all the
rewards of a major literary career that Lamb himself had to forego:

To one like Elia, whose treasures are rather cased in leather covers than closed
in iron coffers, there is a class of alienators more formidable than that which I
have touched upon; I mean your *borrowers of books*—those mutilators of
collections, spoilers of the symmetry of shelves, and creators of odd volumes.
There is Comberbatch, matchless in his depredations![99]

The taking of his books (Comberbatch is of course Coleridge, who had
fled Cambridge as a student and enlisted in the dragoons under the
name of S. T. Comberbache), came to have an openly symbolic
significance for Lamb. 'Why will you make your visits,' he wrote

---

[95] Ibid. 9.   [96] Ibid. 21.   [97] Ibid. 13.   [98] Ibid. 22.   [99] Ibid. 25.

Coleridge in 1820, 'which should give pleasure, matter of regret to your friends? You never come but you take away some folio that is part of my existence.'[100] The essay form that Lamb adopted was suited for someone who had decided to write in prose and compose cabinet curiosities; it was also suited to a man who, because of his labours for the East India Company, had time available only sporadically and in short segments. Happily, however, the form was benign to one of Romanticism's chief insistences, that of the essential oneness of poetry and prose. For if Lamb's essays are a diminished version of the epic venture, they are also specifically parallel to Baudelaire's *Le Spleen de Paris*.

Baudelaire's tiny essays, or 'petits poèmes en prose', as he called them, are by many critics thought to be deeper achievements even than the poems called *Les Fleurs du mal*. At the very opening of his 'petits poèmes en prose', Baudelaire issues a kind of manifesto that tends radically to raise the artistic aspiration of prose essays:

Which of us in his moment of ambition has not dreamed of the miracle of a poetic prose, musical, without rhythm and without rhyme, supple enough and rugged enough to adapt itself to the lyrical impulses of the soul, the undulations of reverie, the jibes of conscience?[101]

In the same preamble Baudelaire makes two further observations that also fit the *Essays of Elia*. 'It was, above all, out of my exploration of huge cities, out of the medley of their innumerable combinations, that this haunting ideal was born.'[102] Such an assertion directly pertains to Lamb's life in the huge city of London. And if the essays as a collection lack form, for Baudelaire as for Lamb that is also their peculiar strength. This work, says Baudelaire, 'has neither head nor tail, since, on the contrary everything in it is both head and tail, alternately and reciprocally. . . . We can cut wherever we please, I my dreaming . . . the reader

---

[100] Lucas, ii. 284. Autumn, 1820. This issue, almost more than any other, threatened to pierce through the tough rind of Lamb's charm. In a letter to Coleridge in 1803, the charm is stretched almost to breaking point: 'By some fatality, unusual with me, I have mislaid the list of books which you want. Can you, from memory, easily supply me with another? I confess to Statius, and I detained him wilfully, out of a reverent regard to your style. Statius, they tell me, is turgid. As to that other Latin book, since you know neither its name nor subject, your wants . . . cannot be very urgent. . . . Your partiality to me has led you to form an erroneous opinion as to the measure of delight you suppose me to take in obliging. . . . Pray, rest more satisfied with the portion of learning which you have got, and disturb my peaceful ignorance as little as possible with such sort of commissions' (Lamb, *Letters*, ii. 116. June 1803).   [101] *Baudelaire*, i. 275–6.   [102] Ibid. 276.

his reading. . . . Chop this fantasy into numerous pieces and you will see that each one can get along alone.'[103]

If the *Essays of Elia*, seen in the matrix of Lamb's subterranean art, exhibit direct similarity to the prestige-filled experiments later undertaken by Baudelaire, they represent on their own terms the great poem of Charles Lamb, a paradoxical fulfilment of those poetic aspirations so early reined in and dismissed. Perhaps their still point of desperation and also of achievement is the essay, 'Dream Children: A Reverie'. This searing little testament of despair, and composition of genius, simultaneously embodies all Lamb's politic virtuosity and expresses his deepest sense of deprivation. One is shocked, despite the charm and the infinitely skilful whimsy, when the loving relationship of Elia to his children, John and Alice, described with such exquisite humanity, dissolves into nothing. It had all been a dream; the return to reality is a return to desolation: 'and immediately awaking, I found myself quietly seated in my bachelor armchair, where I had fallen asleep, with the faithful Bridget unchanged by my side—but John L. (or James Elia) was gone for ever.'[104]

The faithful Bridget, unchanged by his side, was the ever-burdensome Mary, the eternal cross he had to carry.[105] 'I have obligations to Bridget, extending beyond the period of memory,' writes Lamb in 'Mackery End, in Hertfordshire': 'We house together, old bachelor and maid, in a sort of double singleness; with such tolerable comfort, upon the whole, that I, for one, find in my self no sort of disposition to go out upon the mountain . . . to bewail my celibacy.'[106]

There is every reason to think, however, that celibacy was a piteous burden for Lamb to bear. Long before, he had written Coleridge and declared that 'I am wedded . . . to the fortunes of my sister and my poor old father.'[107] Such a wedding allowed no other wife. When in 1819 Lamb proposed marriage to the actress Fanny Kelly, it was specifically to come be a 'reality to us', that is, to Mary as well as to Lamb himself.[108] But the lady was not having any of this; she frankly and decidedly declined the proposal. Nowhere is Lamb's intricate system of defence more evident than in the letter with which he answered her rejection:

Your injunctions shall be obeyed to a tittle. I feel myself in a lackadaisacal no-how-ish kind of a humor. I believe it is the rain, or something. I had thought

---

[103] Ibid. 275.   [104] *Lamb*, ii. 103.

[105] 'I know John will make speeches about it, but she shall not go into an *hospital*' (Lamb, *Letters*, i. 49. 3 Oct. 1796).   [106] *Lamb*, ii. 75.

[107] Lamb, *Letters*, i. 64. 14 Nov. 1796.   [108] Lucas, ii. 254. 20 July 1819.

to have written seriously, but I fancy I succeed best in epistles of mere fun; puns and *that* nonsense. You will be good friends with us, will you not? let what has past 'break no bones' between us.[109]

So Lamb, cast into straitened and almost untenable conditions of life, managed, by complex displacements, to maintain the supports and gain the rewards necessary to survival. His situation was unenviable, at best, and only someone of enormous strength of character could have achieved his special triumph amid the ruins. Despite their profound respect for him, neither Wordsworth nor Coleridge allowed himself to see the full extent of Lamb's struggle. To Wordsworth he was, in the final summing up, 'the frolic and the gentle',[110] while to Coleridge he was 'my gentle-hearted Charles'.[111] To this, Lamb, ever whimsical, could insist on correction: 'In the next edition . . . please to blot out *gentle-hearted*, and substitute drunken dog, ragged-head, seld-shaven, odd-ey'd, stuttering, or any other epithet which truly and properly belongs to the Gentleman in question.'[112] Lamb's later friend, P.G. Patmore, intuited something of the psychic cost at which the frolicsome surface of whimsy was maintained. Behind Lamb's 'pervading sweetness and gentleness', observed Patmore, was the sense that these qualities were 'preserved and persevered in, in spite of opposing and contradictory feelings within, that struggled in vain for mastery'.[113] Karen Horney has poignantly depicted the clinical rage and frustration that inevitably accompany such feelings, and we are accordingly only mildly surprised when Patmore goes on to suggest that Lamb was actually a 'gentle amiable, and tender-hearted misanthrope', and that one part of him 'hated and despised' mankind.[114]

---

[109] Ibid. 255. 20 July 1819. Lamb's system of defence is especially evident in the phrase 'break no bones', which takes up some extended banter of several days before: 'Dear Miss Kelly, If your Bones are not engaged on Monday night, will you favor us with the use of them? I know, if you can oblige us, you will make no bones of it; if you cannot, it shall break none betwixt us. We might ask somebody else, but we do not like the bones of any strange animal. We should be welcome to dear Mrs Liston's, but then she is so plump, there is no getting at them. I should prefer Miss Iver's—they must be ivory I take it for granted—but she is married to Mr XXX, and become bone of his bone, consequently can have none of her own to dispose of. Well, it all comes to this,—if you can let us have them, you will, I dare say; if you cannot, God rest your bones. I am almost at the end of my bon-mots. C. Lamb' (Lucas, ii. 253. 9 July 1819).   [110] Wordsworth, *Poems*, iv. 277.
[111] Coleridge, *Poems*, i. 179.   [112] Lamb, *Letters*, i. 224. 14 Aug. 1800.
[113] Patmore, i. 15–16. Patmore was peculiarly sensitive to the stressful nature of Lamb's existence. 'I appeal to those intimates whether they ever saw Lamb wholly at his ease for half an hour together—wholly free from that restlessness which is incompatible with mental tranquillity' (i. 68–9).   [114] Ibid. 16.

But Lamb's triumph over such forces of disintegration was never in
doubt, and he was held in peculiar honour by his contemporaries, who
sensed the heroic dimension of his constancy even when they did not
precisely formulate it. Boxed in and burdened though he was, he
achieved not simply survival but transcendence. He was, in truth, a
secular saint. 'O, he was good, if e'er a good Man lived!' wrote
Wordsworth.[115] But of the many recognitions of the magnitude of
his spiritual triumph, De Quincey's perhaps gives fullest measure:

I knew Lamb; and I know certain cases in which he was concerned . . . which . . .
would show him to be the very noblest of human beings. He was a man, in a
sense more eminent than would be conceivable by many people, *princely*
—nothing short of that—in his beneficence. Many liberal people I have known
in this world—many who were charitable in the widest sense—many munificent
people; but never any one upon whom, for bounty, for indulgence and forgiveness, for charitable construction of doubtful or mixed actions, and for regal
munificence, you might have thrown yourself with so absolute a reliance as upon
this comparatively poor Charles Lamb. Considered as a man of genius, he was
not in the very first rank, simply because his range was a contracted one: within
that range, he was perfect; of the peculiar powers which he possessed he has left
to the world as exquisite a specimen as this planet is likely to exhibit. But, as a
moral being, in the total compass of his relations to this world's duties, in the
largeness and diffusiveness of his charity, in the graciousness of his condescen-
sion to inferior intellects, I am disposed, after a deliberate review of my own
entire experience, to pronounce him the best man, the nearest in his approaches
to an ideal standard of excellence, that I have known or read of.[116]

To De Quincey's extended encomium we may add, simply and briefly,
that in a special and indeed unique way Charles Lamb was an exemplar
of the high Romantic sensibility, and a hero of existence as well.

[115] Wordsworth, *Poems*, iv. 273.   [116] *De Quincey*, iii. 47–8.

3

The Coarctive Imagination: Hazlitt's Struggle with Coleridge

HAZLITT, like the two other great English essayists of the Romantic era, has been forced out of the cultural mainstream into a still pool at the side of the current. None of the three has undergone any drastic downward revision in reputation, and in a sense their standing, with the possible exception of Lamb, is as high now as, or possibly even higher than, it has ever been. But neither Hazlitt nor Lamb nor De Quincey figures much in large thinkings about their time, nor do they figure much in pedagogic conceivings of what ought to be emphasized in literary instruction for aspiring intellectuals. They have all three been consigned to a kind of limbo of cultural inattention.

The reasons for this curious state of affairs are complex, and not entirely clear. One of them is that all three figures are customarily not included within conceptions of the high Romantic sensibility in England, which is usually reserved for the poets: Wordsworth, Coleridge, Byron, Keats, and Shelley, and, in recent years, Blake. The absence of convenient texts for the essayists has tended, by barring them from university courses in Romanticism, to traditionalize the exclusion. As indicated above, it is one of the main purposes of this volume to readmit them into the Romantic field of cultural force. Hazlitt indeed, as the author of a work, *Liber Amoris*, that can vie with Friedrich Schlegel's *Lucinde* as a key text for Romantic passion, and of a *Life of Napoleon* that could equally well serve as a key text for illustrating Romantic egotism, even on cursory inspection presents impressive Romantic credentials. His consuming passion for Sarah Walker, out of which the *Liber Amoris* grew, is a prime example of that corroding eroticism that Praz described as the romantic agony: '. . . I worshipped her,' said Hazlitt, 'and even now pay her divine honours in my inmost heart, abused and brutalised as I have been by that Circean cup of kisses, of enchantments, of which I have drunk! I am choked, withered, dried up with chagrin, remorse, despair, from which I have not a moment's respite, day or night.'[1]

---

[1] Hazlitt, *Letters*, 279.

Of at least equal importance, however, and far more complex and long-standing in its effect, is the more intricate Romantic index that this chapter will seek to elucidate, that is, Hazlitt's profound intertwinement with a major, and indeed founding, figure of the English Romantic sensibility. That figure is Coleridge.

A second reason for the exclusion of the essayists from the definitions of Romanticism, this reason surely the closest to a kind of poetic justice, is that all three, Hazlitt and De Quincey especially, were so deeply involved with journalistic composition that the whirligig of time brought in its revenges. To write for the journals of the moment meant, in a way, to remain imprisoned within the ephemerality of that moment. The rise of the journals, co-ordinate with the breakdown of patronage and the advent of industrialized society, freed but at the same time entrapped the aspiring writer who did not have a base within the Establishment, whether that base were university appointment or church living or family wealth. It freed him by allowing him the possibility of an honourable income directly earned by the exercise of his talents; it entrapped him by remorselessly forcing his thoughts and his statements to perpetual residence on the surface.[2] An audience must always be pleased if further commissions were to ensue, and further commissions had to ensue if the quotidian demands of bread on the table were to be met. A rather wonderful rendering of this truth occurs in Hazlitt's essay called 'On Living to One's-Self', where the actual event of bread on the table is inextricably linked to the writing thereby necessitated:

I never was in a better place or humour than I am at present for writing on this subject. I have a partridge getting ready for my supper, my fire is blazing on the hearth, the air is mild for this season of the year. . . . I have three hours good before me, and therefore I will attempt it. It is as well to do it at once as to have it to do for a week to come.

If the writing on this subject is no easy task, the thing itself is a harder one. It asks a troublesome effort to ensure the admiration of others: it is a still greater one to be satisfied with one's own thoughts. As I look from the window at the

---

[2] 'With respect to Hazlitt's actual method of composition, he never, I believe, thought for half an hour beforehand, as to what he should say on any given subject . . . but merely, whether it was a subject on which he *had* thought intently at any previous period of his life, and whether it was susceptible of a development that was consistent with the immediate object he might have in view, in sitting down to write on it' (Patmore, iii. 2). 'Hazlitt's method of composition, even on subjects which he was accustomed to treat the most profoundly—moral or metaphysical questions—was rapid, clear, and decisive; so much so in the latter respect, that his MS. was like a fair copy, and he scarcely thought it necessary even to read it over before sending it to the press' (ibid. 11).

wide bare heath before me, and through the misty moon-light air see the woods that wave over the top of Winterslow . . . my mind takes its flight through too long a series of years, supported only by the patience of thought and secret yearnings after truth and good, for me to be at a loss to understand the feeling I intend to write about; but I do not know that this will enable me to convey it more agreeably to the reader.[3]

In that passage we see too another necessity of the journalistic commitment: the author's eye must be constantly and anxiously on the reader; for to displease the reader is eventually to lose livelihood.

The demands of the quotidian and of the surface can be gauged in another way from Hazlitt's preface of 1817 to *The Round Table*:

The following work falls somewhat short of its title and original intention. It was proposed by my friend, Mr Hunt, to publish a series of papers in the Examiner, in the manner of the early periodical Essayists, the Spectator and Tatler. These papers were to be contributed by various persons on a variety of subjects; and Mr Hunt, as the Editor, was to take the characteristic or dramatic part of the work upon himself. I undertook to furnish occasional Essays and Criticisms; one or two other friends promised their assistance; but the essence of the work was to be miscellaneous. The next thing was to fix upon a title for it. After much doubtful consultation, that of THE ROUND TABLE was agreed upon as most descriptive of its nature and design. . . . All the papers, in the two volumes here offered to the public, were written by myself and Mr Hunt, except a letter communicated by a friend in the seventeenth number. Out of the fifty-two numbers, twelve are Mr Hunt's, with the signatures L. H. or H. T. For all the rest I am answerable.[4]

The pressure of the moment resulted in other *ad hoc* forms as well. Hazlitt's *Life of Thomas Holcroft* was written in a few weeks in 1809 from materials placed in his hands by Holcroft's widow. How briskly these materials were heaped up and cobbled together is indicated in a letter from Hazlitt to his father in November 1809:

I have set to pretty hard at Holcroft's Life, and have written (*above*: in the evenings for I paint in the day time) 35 pages in the last week, in addition to near a hundred which I had before transcribed from his own narrative which comes down to his fifteenth year. This will be the best part of the work but I hope to make the rest out tolerably well from memorandums, anecdotes, his own writings, criticisms etc. etc. I shall finish it, I hope, by Christmas, and certainly it will not be a hard job. His own narrative will comprise about 80 quarto pages, in which size it will be printed, a diary which he left for the years 1798 and 99, and which is almost as amusing as Boswell's Life, will take up about 50 more—130,

---

[3] *Hazlitt*, viii. 90.   [4] Ibid. iv. 'Advertisement to the Edition of 1817'.

what I shall write will be about 170 pages, making 300 of the Life, and there will be another 150 pages of letters to and from his friends; in all about 450 pages. Above half the volume will therefore be mere strait forward transcription, and the rest will be merely picking out memorandums etc. from different places, and bringing them together, except such few reflections as I shall have to make, which will not be very long or deep.[5]

Other expression was bound by journalistic exigencies too. Hazlitt's philosophical ambitions, by which he set great store, were discharged into a series of journalistic lectures on the history of English philosophy delivered at the Russell Institution, Great Coram Street, Brunswick Square, from January to April 1812. His *Lectures on the English Poets*, which contain some of his best literary criticism, were delivered at the Surrey Institution, Great Surrey Street, near Blackfriar Bridge, during January and February 1818, and afterwards they were repeated in full at the Crown and Anchor Tavern in the Strand, in April and May of that year. There followed hard upon these a course of lectures on the *English Comic Writers* and immediately after that a course of *Lectures on the Age of Elizabeth*. How intellectually hand-to-mouth this all was may be estimated from Procter's remark about the last-named series:

When [Hazlitt] was about to write his *Lectures on the Age of Elizabeth*, he knew little or nothing of the dramatists of that time, with the exception of Shakespeare. He spoke to Charles Lamb, and to myself, who were supposed by many to be well acquainted with these ancient writers. I lent him about a dozen volumes, comprehending the finest of the old plays; and he then went down to Winterslow Hut, in Wiltshire, and after a stay of six weeks came back to London, fully impregnated with the subject, with his thoughts fully made up on it, and with all his lectures written.[6]

And always there was the constant pouring of print into *The Examiner*, *The Morning Chronicle*, *The Times*, *The Champion*, *The London Magazine*, *The Courier*, *The Edinburgh Review*. Even the work that we now find perhaps his best, *The Spirit of the Age*, appeared in instalments in *The New Monthly Magazine*.

---

[5] Hazlitt, *Letters*, 113.

[6] *Hazlitt*, vi. 385. As Patmore observes of Hazlitt, 'when he had an entire volume of work in hand he invariably went into the country to execute it, and almost always to the same spot—a little wayside public-house, called *The Hut*, standing alone, and some miles distant from any other house, on Winterslow Heath, a barren tract of country on the road to, and a few miles from, Salisbury. There, ensconced in a little wainscoted parlour, looking out over the bare heath to the distant groves of Norman Court, some of his finest essays were written; there, in utter solitude and silence, many of his least unhappy days were spent' (Patmore, iii. 14).

It is idle to speculate what Hazlitt might have been had he been liberated from the constant demands of putting his thoughts down almost as soon as they occurred to him. The expression of those thoughts was, indeed, closely allied to casual conversation. As he says in the 'Advertisement' to the Paris Edition of his *Table Talk; or Original Essays*:

I had remarked that when I had written or thought upon a particular topic, and afterwards had occasion to speak of it with a friend, the conversation generally took a much wider range, and branched off into a number of indirect and collateral questions, which were not strictly connected with the original view of the subject. . . . It therefore occurred to me as possible to combine the advantages of these two styles, the *literary* and *conversational*. . . . This seemed to me to promise a greater variety and richness, and perhaps a greater sincerity, than could be attained by a more precise and scholastic method. The same consideration had an influence on the familiarity and conversational idiom of the style which I have used. . . . I am . . . afraid of having too frequently attempted to give a popular air and effect to subtle distinctions and trains of thought; so that I shall be considered as too metaphysical by the careless reader, while by the more severe and scrupulous inquirer my style will be complained of as too light and desultory. To all this I can only answer that I have done not what I wished, but the best I could do; and I heartily wish it had been better.[7]

That last sentence, 'I have done not what I wished, but the best I could do', might serve as epigraph for the whole of Hazlitt's cultural endeavour.

The best he could do was very good indeed. In truth, he may be the finest pure critic of literature that English culture has brought forth. Certainly he ranks among the most generally acknowledged candidates: Dryden, Dr Johnson, Coleridge, Arnold, Leavis, Empson; and none of these was a pure critic of literature except perhaps for Dryden and Empson, the others all being committed to philosophical, cultural, or moral programmes to which the criticism as such was ancillary. In any case, his prose style, which Hazlitt feared would be complained of as too light and desultory, has rarely elicited complaints from anyone. 'We are mighty fine fellows,' sighed Robert Louis Stevenson, 'but we cannot write like William Hazlitt.'[8] The praise isolates something special about Hazlitt's style, that it is not simply a virtuoso instrument, but a unique one as well. No one has ever written like William Hazlitt; his style, sinewy, direct, and effortless, races along through all topics, those of the

---

[7] *Hazlitt*, viii. 333.   [8] Henley, p. vii.

depths no less than those of the surface, with seemingly no premeditation or striving for effect.

It is a style that has never been analyzed and never imitated, and I shall neither analyze nor imitate it here. Suffice it to say that it is a style that rests upon two elements, an instinct for aphorism and a dazzling command of appositional structure. Unlike the keening cadences of De Quincey's ornate and often-imitated caduceus style, Hazlitt's seems to be composed of minute rhetorical units that slide together in effortless combination towards any topic he wishes to address. He uses few inversions or complex structures. He specializes rather in direct declarative sentences, which he then characteristically lengthens into whatever rhythm he requires by rippling appositional juxtapositions. Not keening cadences but the muted clicks of stainless-steel bearings are the auditory image one grasps for to describe the style of Hazlitt.

It is a style that is peculiarly suited to the virtue that, perhaps more than any other, makes him a great pure critic of literature. That virtue is clear-headedness. Ortega y Gasset, in a memorable discussion, has argued that the rarest of qualities is a clear head; and, indeed, in all of antiquity, he urges, there were only two clear heads: Themistocles and Caesar.[9] There have not been many more since. But Hazlitt must certainly be numbered in the select ranks of those happy few. 'Strange as it may seem,' he once said, in words that indicate the basis of his whole critical procedure, 'to learn what any object is, the true philosopher looks at the object itself, instead of turning to others to know what they think or say or have heard of it, or instead of consulting the dictates of his vanity, petulance, and ingenuity, to see what can be said against their opinion.'[10]

Hazlitt characteristically looked at the object itself, with a clear head, and the results in his literary criticism were judgements of absolute rightness and pregnant condensation of understanding.[11] Consider, for instance, his capsuled statement about Christopher Marlowe, which, despite the existence of many later and often successful studies of that author, remains the standard for Marlowe criticism: 'There is a lust of power in his writings, a hunger and thirst after unrighteousness, a glow

---

[9] José Ortega y Gasset, *The Revolt of the Masses* (New York: W. W. Norton & Company, Inc., 1957 [1930]), 156–7. [10] *Hazlitt*, viii. 147.

[11] Cf. Patmore: 'It was in the astonishing depth and quickness of his first insight into any object of art, that his unequalled critical faculty consisted' (Patmore, iii. 62–3). 'Hazlitt could perceive and describe "at sight" the characteristics of anything, without any previous study or knowledge whatever, but by a species of intellectual intuition' (ibid. 46).

of the imagination, unhallowed by any thing but its own energies.'[12] Of almost equal perceptiveness and condensation is a passing remark about Milton: 'It is rarely that a man even of lofty genius will be able to do more than carry on his own feelings and character ... into fictitious and uncommon situations. Milton has by allusion embodied a great part of his political and personal history in the chief characters and incidents of Paradise Lost.'[13]

He was equally perspicacious in judging his own contemporaries (few can make authoritative judgements without the subliminal support of a prior critical consensus). Of Landor's *Imaginary Conversations*, he observes:

This work is as remarkable an instance as we have lately met with of the strength and weakness of the human intellect. It displays considerable originality, learning, acuteness, terseness of style, and force of invective—but it is spoiled and rendered abortive throughout by an utter want of temper, of self-knowledge, and decorum. Mr Landor's mind is far from barren in feeling or in resources; but over the natural, and (what might be) the useful growth of these, there every where springs up a luxuriant crop of caprice, dogmatism, extravagance, intolerance, quaintness, and most ludicrous arrogance ...[14]

His extended criticism of Landor, in truth, does exactly what Hazlitt thought 'a genuine criticism should': 'reflect the colours, the light and shade, the soul and body of a work.'[15]

By looking at the object rather than consulting the dictates of his vanity or petulance, Hazlitt produced some of the very best criticism of Wordsworth that exists. No one, not Arnold, not even Coleridge himself, saw Wordsworth's genius more clearly and justly, and yet Hazlitt cordially disliked Wordsworth as a person. But he always insisted on Wordsworth's importance and originality:

To the author of the *Lyrical Ballads* nature is a kind of home; and he may be said to take a personal interest in the universe. There is no image so insignificant that it has not in some mood or other found the way into his heart: no sound that does not awaken the memory of other years.... The daisy looks up to him with sparkling eye ... a linnet's nest startles him with boyish delight: an old withered thorn is weighed down with a heap of recollections: a grey cloak, seen on some wild moor, torn by the wind, or drenched in the rain, afterwards becomes an

---

[12] *Hazlitt*, vi. 202.   [13] Ibid. viii. 42.   [14] Ibid. xvi. 240.
[15] Ibid. viii. 217. Conversely, Hazlitt was opposed to the critic whose 'object ... is not to do justice to the author, whom he treats with very little ceremony, but to do himself homage, and to show his acquaintance with all the topics and resources of criticism' (viii. 214).

object of imagination to him: even the lichens on the rocks have a life and being in his thoughts. He has described all these objects in a way and with an intensity of feeling that no one else had done before him. . . . He is in this sense the most original poet now living, and the one whose writings could least be spared: for they have no substitute elsewhere.[16]

In other places Hazlitt says that 'Mr Wordsworth is the most original poet now living';[17] 'Do what he can, he cannot help being an original-minded man';[18] 'He is the greatest, that is, the most original poet of the present day . . .';[19] 'He has opened a new avenue to the human heart, has explored another secret haunt and nook of nature. . . . Compared with his lines, Lord Byron's stanzas are but exaggerated commonplace.'[20]

A concluding witness to Hazlitt's critical clear-headedness and authority may be summoned from a pastiche of statements he made about Shelley's posthumous poems:

'Poetry, we grant, creates a world of its own; but it creates it out of existing materials. Mr Shelley is the maker of his own poetry—out of nothing. Not that he is deficient in the true sources of strength and beauty . . . but . . . he had no respect for any poetry that did not strain the intellect as well as fire the imagination—and was not sublimed into a high spirit of metaphysical philosophy.' 'He was "all air", disdaining the bars and ties of mortal mould.' 'Mr Shelley was a remarkable man. His person was a type and shadow of his genius. His complexion, fair, golden, freckled, seemed transparent with an inward light.' 'Spurning the world of realities, he rushed into the world of nonentities and contingencies, like air into a *vacuum*.' 'It is in his stanza-poetry, that his Muse chiefly runs riot. . . . The *Witch of Atlas*, the *Triumph of Life*, and *Marianne's Dream* . . . abound in horrible imaginings, like records of a ghastly dream;—life, death, genius, beauty, victory, earth, air, ocean, the trophies of the past, the shadows of the world to come, are huddled together in a strange and hurried dance of words, and all that appears clear is the passion and paroxysm of thought of the poet's spirit. The poem entitled the *Triumph of Life*, is in fact a new and terrific *Dance of Death*. . . .'[21]

The clear-headedness of Hazlitt was not confined to literary criticism as such. Most of us customarily plunge through a mental twilight, taking it as normal that we stumble over bushes of misunderstanding, gullies of conventionality, or rocks of fear. But Hazlitt was not hindered by conventionality, or by fear, or by misunderstanding. He saw and calmly reported the emperor's new clothes:

[16] Ibid. xi. 89. [17] Ibid. v. 156. [18] Ibid. viii. 45. [19] Ibid. 44.
[20] Ibid. 45. [21] Ibid. xvi. 265, 266, 268, 269.

The first Methodist on record was David. He was the first eminent person we read of, who made a regular compromise between religion and morality, between faith and good works. After any trifling peccadillo in point of conduct, as a murder, adultery, perjury, or the like, he ascended with his harp into some high tower of his palace; and having chaunted, in a solemn strain of poetical inspiration, the praises of piety and virtue, made his peace with heaven and his own conscience. This extraordinary genius, in the midst of his personal errors retained the same lofty abstract enthusiasm for the favourite objects of his contemplation; the character of the poet and the prophet remained unimpaired by the vices of the man—. . . and the best test of the soundness of his principles and the elevation of his sentiments, is, that they were proof against his practice.[22]

Hazlitt was as clear, direct, and fearless in confronting the Anglican Establishment as he was in assessing biblical religion and Methodism. Of Archdeacon Paley he wrote:

This same shuffling Divine is the same Dr Paley, who afterwards employed the whole of his life, and his moderate second-hand abilities, in tampering with religion, morality and politics,—in trimming between his convenience and his conscience,—in crawling between heaven and earth, and trying to cajole both. His celebrated and popular work on Moral Philosophy is celebrated and popular for no other reason, than that it is a somewhat ingenious and amusing apology for existing abuses of every description. . . . It is a very elaborate and consolatory elucidation of the text, *that men should not quarrel with their bread and butter.* It is not an attempt to show what is right, but to palliate and find out plausible excuses for what is wrong. It is a work without the least value, except as a convenient common-place book or *vade mecum,* for tyro politicians and young divines, to smooth their progress in the Church or the State.[23]

How difficult it was to achieve Hazlitt's sort of directness on biblical matters in nineteenth-century England may be gauged by comparing his statement about David with the early Victorian situation reported by G. M. Young:

Milman, walking through the City early one morning, was held up by a group of porters and made to deliver his opinion: did God really command the Israelites to massacre the people of Canaan? It was the test question. Macaulay . . . wrote that in the Old Testament we read of actions performed by Divine command which without such authority would be atrocious crimes. Lyell . . . called on him and asked him to speak out. He refused. At the height of such a reputation as no other English man of letters has enjoyed, he could not face the storm that would have broken on the head of the infidel who questioned the humanity of Joshua or the veracity of Moses.[24]

[22] Ibid. iv. 47.   [23] Ibid. vii. 252–3.
[24] 'Portrait of an Age,' *Early Victorian England 1830–1865,* ed. G. M. Young (London: Oxford University Press, 1934), ii. 473.

Hazlitt's simple declaration, 'The First Methodist on record was David', witnesses the aphoristic directness of his way of presenting things. That instinct for the aphoristic was most comprehensively indulged by the publication, in 1823, of a work called *Characteristics: in the Manner of Rochefoucault's Maxims*, where he says in the preface that 'I was so struck with the force and beauty of the style and matter' of La Rochefoucauld, 'that I felt an earnest ambition to embody some occasional thoughts of my own in the same form'.[25] He did so, and it was an entirely congenial labour. Indeed, some further statements in the preface pertain not only to the requirements of imitating La Rochefoucauld but also serve as a guide, as it were, to Hazlitt's own practice in developing the aphoristic base of his deadline-ridden journalistic expansions:

There is a peculiar *stimulus* [he says], and at the same time a freedom from all anxiety, in this mode of writing. A thought must tell at once, or not at all. There is no opportunity for considering how we shall make out an opinion by labour and prolixity. An observation must be self-evident; or a reason or illustration (if we give one) must be pithy and concise. Each Maxim should contain the essence or ground-work of a separate Essay, but so developed as of itself to suggest a whole train of reflections to the reader; and it is equally necessary to avoid paradox or common-place. The style also must be sententious and epigrammatic . . .[26]

It was not only the pith and conciseness of La Rochefoucauld that appealed to Hazlitt; he was also in profound sympathy with the French *duc's* cynical view of the world. Hazlitt's considered pessimism about life, in fact, is a second reason, along with his uncanny directness of vision, why the journalistic demands of the moment did not irreparably vitiate the quality of his criticism. Hazlitt knew where he stood; he had looked at life and not found it very impressive; he was not easily betrayed into either rapturous enthusiasm or black despair. His controlled pessimism stood him in good stead, giving him a solid and immovable base, as it were, that took the place of continuous scholarship or meditation, for neither of which had he either the means, the opportunity, or in a sense even the inclination.[27]

---

[25] *Hazlitt*, ix. 165.   [26] Ibid.

[27] De Quincey, who felt a special antipathy to Hazlitt, commented acerbically that 'Hazlitt had read nothing. Unacquainted with Grecian philosophy, with Scholastic philosophy, and with the recomposition of these philosophies in the looms of Germany during the last seventy and odd years, trusting merely to the untrained instincts of keen mother-wit—where should Hazlitt have had the materials for great thinking?' (*De Quincey*, v. 231).

For he took the profession of journalism very seriously, despite all its pressures towards the surface, as a necessary source and bulwark of what Karl Popper calls 'the open society'. 'The French Revolution', said Hazlitt, 'might be described as a remote but inevitable result of the invention of the art of printing.'[28] Hazlitt's reverence for the achievement of that Revolution was scarcely less than Michelet's, and it was the rise of the press that had made it all possible:

The gift of speech, or the communication of thought by words, is that which distinguishes man from other animals. But this faculty is limited and imperfect without the intervention of books, which render the knowledge possessed by every one in the community accessible to all. There is no doubt, then, that the press (as it has existed in modern times) is the great organ of intellectual improvement and civilization.[29]

More specifically, the press, for the committedly libertarian Hazlitt, was the surest means of diluting the power of tyrants large and small. He draws a vivid picture of the situation that obtains 'as long as there was no common standard or impartial judge to appeal to; and this could only be found in public opinion, the offspring of books'. He continues:

As long as any unjust claim or transaction was confined to the knowledge of the parties concerned, the tyrant and the slave, which is the case in all unlettered states of society, *might* must prevail over *right*; for the strongest would bully, and the weakest must submit, even in his own defence, and persuade himself that he was in the wrong even in his own despite: but the instant the world (that dread jury) are impanelled, and called to look on and be umpires in the scene, so that nothing is done by connivance or in a corner, then reason mounts the judgment-seat in lieu of passion or interest, and opinion becomes law, instead of arbitrary will; and farewell feudal lord and sovereign king![30]

The energies dissipated in journalism were therefore, in Hazlitt's view of political desirability, properly expended, and his controlled pessimism consequently had to serve philosophically in lieu of constant meditative rethinkings of particular issues. Combined with his clarity of vision it served well. If we ask where such controlled pessimism is manifest, the answer is, everywhere. A fittingly aphoristic presentation of it begins an essay entitled 'On Pedantry': 'Life is the art of being well deceived; and in order that the deception may succeed, it must be habitual and uninterrupted.'[31] If we seek an expanded statement, we may turn to the effortless paragraph that concludes his *Lectures on the Age of Elizabeth*:

[28] *Hazlitt*, xiii. 38.   [29] Ibid.   [30] Ibid. 40.   [31] Ibid. iv. 84.

In youth we borrow patience from our future years: the spring of hope gives us courage to act and suffer. A cloud is upon our onward path, and we fancy that all is sunshine beyond it. The prospect seems endless, because we do not know the end of it. We think that life is long, because art is so, and that, because we have much to do, it is well worth doing: or that no exertions can be too great, no sacrifices too painful, to overcome the difficulties we have to encounter. Life is a continued struggle to be what we are not, and to do what we cannot. But as we approach the goal, we draw in the reins; the impulse is less, as we have not so far to go; as we see objects nearer, we become less sanguine in the pursuit: it is not the despair of not attaining, so much as knowing there is nothing worth obtaining, and the fear of having nothing left even to wish for, that damps our ardour, and relaxes our efforts; and if the mechanical habit did not increase the facility, would, I believe, take away all inclination or power to do any thing. We stagger on the few remaining paces to the end of our journey; make perhaps one final effort; and are glad when the task is done.[32]

Hazlitt's controlled pessimism, to take one further example that can serve as transition to other concerns, permeates his remarkable essay, 'On the Feeling of Immortality in Youth'. 'No young man believes he shall ever die'. That is the opening sentence, and the essay progresses, with imperturbable calmness, to a stark view of the transitoriness of all existence.[33] Emphatically Hazlitt sees that age as best which is the first, when youth and blood are warmer:

To be young is to be as one of the Immortal Gods. . . . Death, old age, are words without a meaning, that pass by us like the idle air which we regard not. . . . We look round in a new world, full of life, and motion, and ceaseless progress; and feel in ourselves all the vigour and spirit to keep pace with it, and do not foresee from any present symptoms how we shall be left behind in the natural course of things, decline into old age, and drop into the grave.[34]

Equably but insistently Hazlitt looks at the paradox of human existence in a way that we consistently mask from our own thoughts:

To see the golden sun and the azure sky, the outstretched ocean, to walk upon the green earth . . . to traverse desert wilderness, to listen to the midnight choir, to visit lighted halls, or plunge into the dungeon's gloom, or sit in crowded theatres and see life itself mocked, to feel heat and cold, pleasure and pain, right and wrong, truth and falsehood, to study the works of art and refine the sense of beauty to agony, to worship fame and to dream of immortality, to have read Shakespear and belong to the same species as Sir Isaac Newton; to be and to do all this, and then in a moment to be nothing . . . there is something revolting and incredible to sense in the transition, and no wonder that, aided by youth and

[32] Ibid. vi. 364.   [33] Ibid. xvii. 189.   [34] Ibid. 190.

warm blood, and the flush of enthusiasm, the mind contrives for a long time to reject it with disdain and loathing as a monstrous and improbable fiction.[35]

The passage above, with all its rippling appositions, and in a form, moreover, that has been shortened for inclusion in this chapter, is nevertheless a single sentence; and it is a good example of one of Hazlitt's effortless stylistic expansions.

And yet the great stylist is frequently unfocused, and in a special way that leads us, I believe, to understand something unique about his intellectual activity. Hazlitt wrote to Leigh Hunt that 'You say I want imagination. If you mean invention or fancy, I say so too; but if you mean a disposition to sympathise with the claims or merits of others, I deny it.'[36] The imaginative limitation here described is, however, further limited by the unique characteristic just referred to. I call this unique characteristic Hazlitt's coarctive imagination. Through an awareness of its function one may be able to approach more rewardingly than other commentators have the supreme mental relationship of his life, that with Coleridge.

By the phrase 'coarctive imagination' is designated a tendency, restricted to Hazlitt alone, to express his sympathy or antipathy with the claims or merits of others in two different and discrete ways rather than in one unified way. This divided expression can occur either simultaneously, which is the case with the stylistic flaws mentioned above, or alternatively, as is the case with many of Hazlitt's critical judgements. The coarctive imagination, one surmises, is generated by the presence, on the one hand, of the extreme clarity of Hazlitt's vision allied to the immediate demands of the topics addressed by his journalistic commitments, and, on the other, by the presence of all the reservations, ambiguities, second thoughts, and recognitions of subsidiary or alternative possibilities that naturally occupy the attention of anyone as extraordinarily intelligent as Hazlitt was. With other writers—De Quincey is a fair example—the reservations, shadings, ambiguities, and qualifications are almost the essence of the style, and are constantly implied in rhetorical subordinations conveyed by the very structure of discourse. *A fortiori* this holds true of the ruminative style of Coleridge, which

---

[35] Ibid. 192–4.

[36] Hazlitt, *Letters*, 206. 21 Apr. 1821. Cf. Talfourd's comment on Hazlitt's mind: 'Acute, fervid, vigorous, as his mind was, it wanted the one great central power of Imagination, which brings all the other faculties into harmonious action' (Talfourd, ii. 158).

snakes through endless parenthetical asides and subordinated qualifications on its progress towards meaning, and sometimes eddies away
inconclusively before meaning is reached, or at least before the reader
has reached it. With Hazlitt, however, the condition of effortless
appositional expansion is possible only by saying just one thing clearly
and directly, a sole and single thing. No one was ever less murky,
tentative, or obfuscatory than Hazlitt: this is the glory and at the same
time the limitation of his mode of expression.

Such direct clarity of style can lend itself either to alternating
emphases or to superimposed emphases. These latter result in the
paradox noted above, that the great stylist frequently seems unfocused.
The most dramatic and constant expression of this lack of focus, and one
that without an understanding of the coarctive imagination is entirely
baffling, is Hazlitt's habit of continually interposing poetic quotations,
usually ranging from two or three words to two or three lines, into his
prose discourse.[37] These poetic interpolations are remarkable for their
frequency, for their inaccuracy, and for their irrelevance.[38] They are
usually less elegant than his own prose statement, and they generally act
to muddy the meaning rather than to enhance it.[39] They can best be
described in their effect if one thinks of a double image on a television
screen, which results from two different signals being picked up at the
same time. The poetical quotations are almost always cast in the form of
appositional statements, and they can invariably be removed with no

---

[37] 'There is another vice in Mr Hazlitt's mode of composition, viz. the habit of trite
quotation, too common to have challenged much notice. . . . To have the verbal memory
infested with tags of verse and "cues" of rhyme is in itself an infirmity as vulgar and as
morbid as the stable-boy's habit of whistling slang airs upon the mere mechanical
excitement of a bar or two whistled by some other blockhead in some other stable' (De
Quincey, v. 236–7).

[38] For an argument that the quotations, on the contrary, actually enrich Hazlitt's prose,
see Jonathan Bate, 'Hazlitt's Shakespearean Quotations', Prose Studies, 7 (1984), 26–37.
About the frequency of the quotations, however, there can be no argument; Bate, indeed,
supplies the following remarkable accounting: 'Setting aside references where Hazlitt is
discussing some specific point in Shakespeare, there are over two thousand four hundred
quotations from the plays and sonnets in P. P. Howe's edition of the Complete Works.
Hazlitt quotes from a wide range of authors; the second highest frequency belongs to
Milton, but the total number of Miltonic phrases is outweighed by those (over five
hundred) from Hamlet alone. Second to Hamlet is Macbeth, quoted over three hundred
times; Othello, which must have had special poignancy for the Hazlitt of Liber Amoris,
occurs about two hundred and fifty times, As You Like It and 1 Henry IV each just over a
hundred. The only play from which Hazlitt does not quote is 1 Henry VI' (26).

[39] Talfourd felt that Hazlitt 'frequently diminished the immediate effect of his reason-
ings by the prodigality and richness of the allusions with which he embossed them'
(Talfourd, ii. 157).

damage to the sense of the larger passage. Indeed, this fact of itself testifies to their being of a nature alien to the primary discourse.

Inasmuch as the lengthy passages quoted in this chapter almost always replace these quotations by ellipses, my readers can have no sense of their frequency or disruptiveness. It is necessary, therefore, to provide an example of their prevalence, but I shall restrict myself to only one. Writing in proleptic censure of Coleridge's *Lay Sermon*,[40] Hazlitt says:

He has all the faculties of the human mind but one, and yet without that one, the rest only impede and interfere with each other—'Like to a man on double business bound who both neglects.' He would have done better if he had known less. His imagination thus becomes metaphysical, his metaphysics fantastical, his wit heavy, his arguments light, his poetry prose, his prose poetry, his politics turned—but not to account. He belongs to all parties and is of service to none. He gives up his independence of mind, and yet does not acquire independence of fortune. He offends others without satisfying himself, and equally by his servility and singularity, shocks the prejudices of all about him. If he had had but common moral principle, that is, sincerity, he would have been a great man; nor hardly, as it is, appears to us—

'Less than arch-angel ruined, and the excess Of glory obscur'd.'

We lose our patience when we think of the powers that he has wasted, and compare them and their success with those, for instance, of such a fellow as the——, all whose ideas notions, apprehensions, comprehensions, feelings, virtues, genius, skill, are comprised in the two words which *Peachum* describes as necessary qualifications in his gang, 'To stand himself and bid others stand!'[41]

This is a fair example of Hazlitt's customary practice. If we ask why such a supreme stylist obstructs his own mastery, a conjectural answer presents itself. Hazlitt, except for his genius, was a kind of Jude the Obscure. The disadvantaged youth, 'dumb, inarticulate, helpless', as he described himself, is in the poetic quotations reaching out of his 'original bondage, dark, obscure, with longings infinite and unsatisfied', for the respectability of culture.[42] Certainly in the poetic quotations he seems forever to be trying to load every rift with ore, in the hope that the glitter will qualify him to those who had the university education he himself was denied. That the lack of such education rankled deeply seems to be the intertext, as it were, of his searing essay 'On the

---

[40] The review, wickedly, was written *before* the book appeared.
[41] *Hazlitt*, vii. 117–18.   [42] Ibid. xvii. 107.

Ignorance of the Learned'. 'Any one', he says, 'who has passed through the regular gradations of a classical education, and is not made a fool by it, may consider himself as having had a very narrow escape.'[43] He contemptuously dismisses 'the learned pedant', who

is conversant with books only as they are made of other books, and those again of others, without end. He parrots those who have parroted others. He can translate the same word into ten different languages, but he knows nothing of the *thing* which it means in any one of them. He stuffs his head with authorities built on authorities, with quotations quoted from quotations, while he locks up his senses, his understanding, and his heart. . . . The language of nature, or of art (which is another nature), is one that he does not understand. He repeats indeed the names of Apelles and Phidias, because they are to be found in classic authors, and boasts of their works as prodigies, because they no longer exist; or, when he sees the finest remains of Grecian art actually before him in the Elgin marbles, takes no other interest in them than as they lead to a learned dispute, and (which is the same thing) a quarrel about the meaning of a Greek particle. He is equally ignorant of music; he 'knows no touch of it', from the strains of the all-accomplished Mozart to the shepherd's pipe upon the mountain. His ears are nailed to his books; and deadened with the sound of the Greek and Latin tongues, and the din and smithery of school-learning. Does he know any thing more of poetry? He knows the number of feet in a verse, and of acts in a play; but of the soul or spirit he knows nothing. He can turn a Greek ode into English, or a Latin epigram into Greek verse, but whether either is worth the trouble, he leaves to the critics.[44]

This sort of schooling Hazlitt lacked, and though his thrusts go deep, a special force is imparted to them by his feeling of deprivation.[45] The poetic quotations, one surmises, compensate for this cultural deprivation; their urgency arises from a different area of Hazlitt's mind and experience than the discourses in which they are embedded.

Be that as it may, the poetical quotations are as frequent in their occurrence as they are detachable and alien in their imaginative origin. They represent the coarctive imagination in its simultaneous presen-

---

[43] Ibid. viii. 71.   [44] Ibid. 73–4.

[45] The force of his appeal to living experience is impressive: 'A lad with a sickly constitution, and not very active; who can just retain what is pointed out to him, and has neither sagacity to distinguish nor spirit to enjoy for himself, will generally be at the head of his form. An idler at school, on the other hand, is one who has high health and spirits, who has the free use of his limbs, with all his wits about him, who feels the circulation of his blood and the motion of his heart, who is ready to laugh and cry in a breath, and who had rather chase a ball or a butterfly, feel the open air in his face, look at the fields or the sky, follow a winding path . . . than doze over a musty spelling-book . . . and receive his reward for the loss of time and pleasure in paltry prize-medals at Christmas and Midsummer' (*Hazlitt*, viii. 72).

tation of discrete and separated concerns, and they relate primarily to the style of Hazlitt's utterance. On the other hand, the second mode of the coarctive imagination's employment relates mainly to the substance of his criticism. In this mode Hazlitt tends to say one thing, directly and effortlessly, while holding back all reservations, qualifications, contradictions, and second thoughts for an entirely different occasion. The technique allows him great power and suppleness of expression at the same time as it can mislead the cursory reader into thinking he understands Hazlitt's mind on a given topic, when in fact only one aspect of Hazlitt's mind is being expressed.

The matter is important. For a single illustration, consider the opening of Hazlitt's essay on the British politician Canning:

Mr Canning was the cleverest boy at Eton: he is, perhaps, the cleverest man in the House of Commons. It is, however, in the sense in which, according to Mr Wordsworth, 'the child is father to the man'. He has grown up entirely out of what he then was. He has merely ingrafted a set of Parliamentary phrases and the technicalities of debate on the themes and school-exercises he was set to compose as a boy. Nor has he ever escaped from the trammels imposed on youthful genius: he has never assumed a manly independence of mind. He has been all his life in the habit of getting up a speech at the nod of a Minister, as he used to get up a thesis under the direction of his school-master.[46]

Now this, we all no doubt agree, is highly effective prose. It skewers Canning directly and cleanly. It says, however, only one thing. There must be more and other things to say about Canning, other sides to his character and import, but the condition that generates Hazlitt's effect is that he should not detract from the force of the expression by considering ambiguities. Thus it is that a hundred words later Hazlitt is still brilliant but still saying only one thing: 'His reasoning is a tissue of glittering sophistry; his language is a cento of florid common-places.'[47] Skip another hundred words, and the force and texture are the same:

. . . he is a mere House-of-Commons man, or, since he was transferred there from College, appears never to have seen or thought of any other place. He may be said to have passed his life in making and learning to make speeches. All other objects and pursuits seem to have been quite lost upon him. He has overlooked the ordinary objects of nature, the familiar interests of human life, as beneath his notice.[48]

---

[46] Hazlitt, xi. 150. Canning is clearly a variant of the young pedant scorned by Hazlitt above.   [47] Ibid. 151.   [48] Ibid.

Should Hazlitt wish to say other kinds of things about Canning, he must either give up the appositional ease of his stylistic expansion, or, and this is what he tends to do, simply find another occasion on which to say the other things. His treatment of Burke, who was, next to Coleridge, the most important figure in his intellectual background, precisely reveals this tendency. On the one hand, Hazlitt venerated Burke as a great thinker and great man, and as the finest stylist that English prose had produced; but he was radically at odds with Burke's political conservatism. So he produces two portraits of Burke, one painted in words of unstinting admiration, and the other quite different. In an essay of 1807, Hazlitt writes of Burke:

... there is no single speech which can convey a satisfactory idea of his powers of mind: to do him justice, it would be necessary to quote all his works: the only specimen of Burke is, *all that he wrote*... The only limits which circumscribed his variety were the stores of his own mind. His stock of ideas did not consist of a few meagre facts, meagrely stated, of half a dozen common-places tortured in a thousand different ways: but his mine of wealth was a profound understanding, inexhaustible as the human heart and various as the sources of nature. He therefore enriched every subject to which he applied himself, and new subjects were only the occasions of calling forth fresh powers of mind which had not been before exerted. It would therefore be in vain to look for the proof of his powers in any one of his speeches or writings: they all contain some additional proof of power.[49]

This tone of intense and level admiration is maintained throughout the essay. Further on Hazlitt says:

I am not going to make an idle panegyric on Burke (he has no need of it): but I cannot help looking upon him as the chief boast and ornament of the English House of Commons. What has been said of him is, I think, strictly true, that 'he was the most eloquent man of his time: his wisdom was greater than his eloquence.' The only public man that in my opinion can be put in any competition with him, is Lord Chatham. . . . Chatham's eloquence was popular: his wisdom was altogether plain and practical. Burke's eloquence was that of the poet; of the man of high and unbounded fancy: his wisdom was profound and contemplative. Chatham's eloquence was calculated to make men *act*; Burke's was calculated to make them *think*. . . . In research, in originality, in variety of knowledge, in richness of invention, in depth and comprehension of mind, Burke had as much the advantage of Lord Chatham as he was excelled by him in plain common sense, in strong feeling, in steadiness of purpose, in vehemence, in warmth, in enthusiasm, and energy of mind. Burke was the man of genius, of fine sense, and subtle reasoning; Chatham was a man of clear understanding, of

[49] Ibid. vii. 301.

strong sense, and violent passions. . . . That power which governed Burke's mind was his Imagination; that which gave its *impetus* to Chatham's was Will.[50]

In this characterization of Burke, adverse criticism is almost entirely held back. Some ten years later, however, Hazlitt wrote another character of Burke in which the coarctive imagination moved from systolic praise to diastolic denigration:

It is not without reluctance that we speak of the vices and infirmities of such a mind as Burke's. . . . Mr Burke, the opponent of the American war, and Mr Burke, the opponent of the French Revolution, are not the same person, but opposite persons—not opposite persons only, but deadly enemies. In the latter period, he abandoned not only all his practical conclusions, but all the principles on which they were founded. . . . In the American war, he constantly spoke of the rights of the people as inherent, and inalienable: after the French Revolution, he began by treating them with the chicanery of a sophist, and ended by raving at them with the fury of a maniac.[51]

And Hazlitt goes on to say, in direct opposition to the praise of his earlier characterization, that,

The truth is, that Burke was a man of fine fancy and subtle reflection; but not of sound and practical judgment, nor of high or rigid principles.—As to his understanding, he certainly was not a great philosopher; for his works of mere abstract reasoning are shallow and inefficient:—nor was he a man of sense and business; for, both in counsel, and in conduct, he alarmed his friends as much at least as his opponents. . . .[52]

That the coarctive imagination was a recurring feature of Hazlitt's intellectual stance, and not a merely accidental disposition of mind can be seen, to cite one more example, in his judgements of the poet Thomas Campbell. In *The Spirit of the Age*, Hazlitt speaks of Campbell in terms of high praise:

The author of the *Pleasures of Hope*, with a richer and deeper vein of thought and imagination, works it out into figures of equal grace and dazzling beauty, avoiding on the one hand the tinsel of flimsy affectation, and on the other the vices of a rude and barbarous negligence. . . . Mr Campbell gives scope to his feelings and his fancy, and embodies them in a noble and naturally interesting subject. . . . The character of his mind is a lofty and self-scrutinising ambition, that strives to reconcile the integrity of general design with the perfect elaboration of each component part. . . . We should dread to point out (even if we could) a false concord, a mixed metaphor, an imperfect rhyme, in any of Mr Campbell's productions: for we think that all his fame would hardly compensate to him for

---

[50] Ibid. 302–3.   [51] Ibid. 226.   [52] Ibid. 227.

the discovery. He seeks for perfection, and nothing evidently short of it can satisfy his mind.[53]

Hazlitt speaks in particularly glowing tones of Campbell's *Gertrude of Wyoming*: 'there are passages in the *Gertrude of Wyoming*', he says, 'of so rare and ripe a beauty, that they challenge, as they exceed all praise.'[54] After quoting one such passage at length, he says:

In the foregoing stanzas we particularly admire the line—

> Till now, in Gertrude's eyes, their ninth blue
> summer shone.

It appears to us like the ecstatic union of natural beauty and poetic fancy, and in its playful sublimity resembles the azure canopy mirrored in the smiling waters, bright, liquid, serene, heavenly! . . . There are other parts of this poem equally delightful, in which there is a light startling as the red-bird's wing; a perfume like that of the magnolia; a music like the murmuring of pathless woods or of the everlasting notes.[55]

This, we might agree, all seems so extravagant that we hardly know what to make of it, especially if we have previously agreed with Keats that one of the wonders of the age was Hazlitt's depth of taste.[56] But the extravagance is more an effect of the shapings of the coarctive imagin-ation than a failure of taste as such. In his *Lectures on the English Poets* Hazlitt speaks of Campbell in terms antithetical to the praise just quoted, and in terms, moreover, that are much closer to what we today think: 'Campbell's Pleasures of Hope', he says,

is of the same school, in which a painful attention is paid to the expression in proportion as there is little to express, and the decomposition of prose is substituted for the composition of poetry. How much the sense and keeping in the ideas are sacrificed to a jingle of words and epigrammatic turn of expressions, may be seen in such lines as the following—

and Hazlitt then proceeds to quote and dissect a passage.[57] He continues with his cold assessment of Campbell's poetry:

His verses on the Battle of Hohenlinden have considerable spirit and animation. His Gertrude of Wyoming is his principal performance. It is a kind of historical paraphrase of Mr Wordsworth's poem of Ruth. It shews little power, or power enervated by extreme fastidiousness. . . . Mr Campbell always seem to me to be

---

[53] Ibid. xi. 159–60.   [54] Ibid. 161.   [55] Ibid. 162.

[56] 'I am convinced that there are three things to rejoice at in this Age—The Excursion, Your [Haydon's] Pictures, and Hazlitt's depth of Taste' (Keats, *Letters*, i. 203). 'I said if there were three things superior in the modern world, they were "the Excursion", "Haydon's pictures" & "Hazlitt's depth of Taste"' (ibid. 204–5).

[57] *Hazlitt*, v. 149.

thinking how his poetry will look when it comes to be hot-pressed on superfine wove paper, to have a disproportionate eye to points and commas, and dread of errors of the press. He is so afraid of doing wrong, of making the smallest mistake, that he does little or nothing. Lest he should wander irretrievably from the right path, he stands still. He writes according to established etiquette. He offers the Muses no violence. If he lights upon a good thought, he immediately drops it for fear of spoiling a good thing. . . . He plays the hypercritic on himself, and starves his genius to death from a needless apprehension of a plethora. No writer who thinks habitually of the critics, either to tremble at their censures or set them at defiance, can write well. It is the business of reviewers to watch poets, not of poets to watch reviewers. . . . The love-scenes in Gertrude of Wyoming breathe a balmy voluptuousness of sentiment; but they are generally broken off in the middle. . . . There is another fault in this poem, which is the mechanical structure of the fable. The most striking events occur in the shape of antitheses. The story is cut into the form of a parallelogram.[58]

The coarctive imagination has required this rather extended illustration as the necessary preliminary to a consideration of the role of Coleridge in Hazlitt's intellectual background. Without an awareness that his coarctive imagination allows Hazlitt to tell the truth directly and powerfully at the same time that it rarely allows any statement to be the full revelation of his mind on the subject at issue, we are likely to misinterpret what Coleridge meant to him, and are almost certain to fail to grasp the weight, texture, and nuance of that relationship. Coleridge was the Bloomean strong precursor for all of Hazlitt's effort; not to see the struggle between them clearly is not to see Hazlitt clearly. Yet in previous commentaries there has been a consistently distorting tendency to see only one aspect of Hazlitt's tropism towards his somewhat older contemporary. 'Many a critic deemed original', wrote William Maginn in 1833, 'has lived exclusively by sucking Coleridge's brains. The late William Hazlitt was one of the most conspicuous thieves. There was not an observation—not a line—in all Hazlitt's critical works, which was worth reading, or remembering, that did not emanate directly from our old friend the Platonist . . .'.[59]

The statement contains an element of truth, but it constitutes a grievous misconception of the whole truth.[60] And yet we may well

---

[58] Ibid. 149–50.

[59] [William Maginn], 'Gallery of Literary Characters', No. xxxviii, Fraser's Magazine, 8 (July 1833), 64.

[60] Patmore observed indignantly that 'precisely because [Hazlitt] was the most original thinker of his day, we heard him held up as a mere waiter upon the intellectual wealth of his literary acquaintance—a mere sucker of the brains of Charles Lamb and Coleridge' (Patmore, ii. 348).

wonder if it constitutes a more serious distortion than do the arguments of the modern scholar David Bromwich in his recent book on Hazlitt. Though Bromwich's volume may be the best, and is certainly the most elegant, of modern studies of Hazlitt, and though one applauds its lengthy, subtle, and devoted attempt to restore Hazlitt to the forefront of our consciousness, praise must be withheld from its treatment of the relationship between Hazlitt and Coleridge. Everywhere it seeks to minimize the importance of that relationship. Ever trying to raise Hazlitt, the volume repeatedly denigrates Coleridge. A single example taken at random will serve to illustrate the tone and technique of the discussion in all its permutations. Hazlitt, says Bromwich, 'argues as a thinking disciple of Hume. Coleridge despised Hume, without giving clear evidence that he had read or understood him.'[61] But Hazlitt himself does not doubt Coleridge's reading or understanding, merely his fairness. In amplified and ramified instances, this is the tone and attitude that permeate Bromwich's book.[62] Knife at the ready, Bromwich experiences no hesitation before the Gordian entanglement of Hazlitt's relation to Coleridge.

Yet neither stance will do. Neither the viewpoint of Bromwich nor that of Maginn is the true perspective on Hazlitt; both mistake a part of Hazlitt for the whole. How easy this is to do, without an understanding of the prevalence of the coarctive imagination in Hazlitt's writings, may be shown by comparing Hazlittian opinions about Coleridge and about Burke. Hazlitt is here writing in an essay called 'On the Prose Style of Poets', and his opinions on style are particularly welcome in view of the large importance this chapter has placed on his own style. First, his remarks on Coleridge's style:

I am indebted to Mr Coleridge for the comparison of poetic prose to the second-hand finery of a lady's maid. . . . He himself is an instance of his own observation, and (what is even worse) of the opposite fault—an affectation of quaintness and originality. With bits of tarnished lace and worthless frippery, he assumes a sweeping oriental costume, or borrows the stiff dresses of our ancestors, or starts an eccentric fashion of his own. He is swelling and turgid—everlastingly aiming to be greater than his subject; filling his fancy with fumes and vapours in the pangs and throes of miraculous parturition, and bringing forth only *still births*. He has an incessant craving, as it were, to exalt every idea into a metaphor, to expand every sentiment into a lengthened mystery, voluminous and vast, confused and cloudy. His style is not succinct, but

---

[61] David Bromwich, *Hazlitt: The Mind of a Critic* (New York: Oxford University Press, 1983), 18.   [62] e.g., 14, 19, 20, 55, 233, 235, 236–7, 253, 432.

incumbered with a train of words and images that have no practical, and only a possible relation to one another—that add to its stateliness, but impede its march. One of his sentences winds its 'forlorn way obscure' over the page like a patriarchal procession with camels laden, wreathed turbans, household wealth, the whole riches of the author's mind poured out upon the barren waste of his subject.... All this is owing to his wishing to overdo every thing—to make something more out of everything than it is, or than it is worth. The simple truth does not satisfy him—no direct proposition fills up the moulds of his understanding.[63]

These are hard knocks indeed, and they hit their target cleanly. They invite contrast with what Hazlitt says about Burke's style in the same essay:

It has always appeared to me that the most perfect prose-style, the most powerful, the most dazzling, the most daring, that which went the nearest to the verge of poetry, and yet never fell over, was Burke's. It has the solidity, and sparkling effect of the diamond: all other *fine writing* is like French paste or Bristol-stones in the comparison. Burke's style is airy, flighty, adventurous, but it never loses sight of the subject; nay, it is always in contact with, and derives its increased or varying impulse from it.... It differs from poetry, as I conceive, like the chamois from the eagle: it climbs to an almost equal height ... but all the while, instead of soaring through the air, it stands upon a rocky cliff, clambers up by abrupt and intricate ways, and browzes on the roughest bark, or crops the tender flower. The principle which guides his pen is truth, not beauty—not pleasure, but power.[64]

If one should read only this encomium, one would think Hazlitt had nothing but praise for Burke; however, as we have seen above, his full opinion contained almost as much criticism as praise, perhaps even more. The same structure obtains with the passage just quoted about Coleridge. If we took it in isolation, we might conclude that Hazlitt held Coleridge in contempt. The inference would be no more valid than the contrary one for Burke.

Though Hazlitt frequently speaks of Coleridge contemptuously he was far from holding him in contempt.[65] The whole truth is that Hazlitt thought Coleridge the greatest mind of the age, and yet the most

---

[63] *Hazlitt*, xii. 15. Elsewhere Hazlitt says that Coleridge 'moves in an unaccountable diagonal between truth and falsehood, sense and nonsense, sophistry and common-place.... A matter of fact is abhorrent to his nature.... Two things are indispensable to him—to set out from no premise, and to arrive at no conclusion' (ibid. vii. 116).

[64] *Ibid.* xii, 10.

[65] On the contrary, as Patmore observed, Hazlitt 'exaggerated his estimate of the intellectual powers of that extraordinary man to an almost superhuman pitch' (Patmore, iii. 148).

disappointing. He considered Coleridge the most brilliant man he had ever known, but the one who had done least to justify that brilliance. But always, from first to last, there was a substratum of awe-struck admiration.[66] The structure is dramatically clear in a virtuoso passage in *The Spirit of the Age*, where massive and bedazzled wonderment is succeeded by dry disappointment. The praise, indeed, which is in the form of an assessment of Coleridge's intellectual biography, constitutes a rhetorical summit of English prose, for it is not only the most magnificent single example of appositional expansion our entire literature affords, but is, almost unbelievably, a single sentence in its structure. Hazlitt has been speaking of Coleridge's conversational prowess, and he has concluded with terms of unalloyed praise:

> One of the finest and rarest parts of Mr Coleridge's conversation, is when he expatiates on the Greek tragedians (not that he is not well acquainted, when he pleases, with the epic poets, or the philosophers, or orators, or historians of antiquity)—on the subtle reasonings and melting pathos of Euripides, on the harmonious gracefulness of Sophocles . . . on the high-wrought trumpet-tongued eloquence of Aeschylus. . . . As the impassioned critic speaks and rises in his theme, you would think you heard the voice of the Man hated by the Gods, contending with the wild winds as they roar, and his eye glitters with the spirit of Antiquity:[67]

And then follows the memorable sentence, which courses like a river through two full pages:

> Next, [writes Hazlitt] he was engaged with Hartley's tribes of mind, 'etherial braid, thought-woven,'—and he busied himself for a year or two with vibrations and vibratiuncles and the great law of association that binds all things in its mystic chain, and the doctrine of Necessity (the mild teacher of Charity) and the Millennium, anticipative of a life to come—and he plunged deep into the controversy on Matter and Spirit, and, as an escape from Dr Priestley's Materialism, where he felt himself imprisoned by the logician's spell, like Ariel in the cloven pine-tree, he became suddenly enamoured of Bishop Berkeley's fairy-world, and used in all companies to build the universe, like a brave poetical fiction, of fine words—and he was deep-read in Malebranche, and in Cudworth's Intellectual System (a huge pile of learning, unwieldy, enormous) and in Lord Brook's hieroglyphic theories, and in Bishop Butler's Sermons, and in the Duchess of Newcastle's fantastic folios, and in Clarke and South and

---

[66] Cf. Patmore 'I can call to mind only one person for whom Hazlitt seemed habitually to entertain a sentiment of personal kindness and esteem, and one only (among his contemporaries) for whose intellectual powers he felt and uniformly expressed a general deference and respect. The first of these was Charles Lamb, the second was Coleridge' (Patmore, ii. 327).　　[67] *Hazlitt*. xi. 31–2.

Tillotson, and all the fine thinkers and masculine reasoners of that age—and Leibnitz's *Pre-Established Harmony* reared its arch above his head, like the rainbow in the cloud, covenanting with the hopes of man—and then he fell plump, ten thousand fathoms down (but his wings saved him harmless) into the *hortus siccus* of Dissent, where he pared religion down to the standard of reason and stripped faith of mystery, and preached Christ crucified and the Unity of the Godhead, and so dwelt for a while in the spirit with John Huss and Jerome of Prague and Socinus and old John Zisca, and ran through Neal's History of the Puritans, and Calamy's Non-Conformists' Memorial, having like thoughts and passions with them—but then Spinoza became his God, and he took up the vast chain of being in his hand, and the round world became the centre and the soul of all things in some shadowy sense, forlorn of meaning, and around him he beheld the living traces and the sky-pointing proportions of the mighty Pan —but poetry redeemed him from this spectral philosophy, and he bathed his heart in beauty, and gazed at the golden light of heaven, and drank of the spirit of the universe, and wandered at eve by fairy-stream or fountain . . . and wedded with truth in Plato's shade, and in the writings of Proclus and Plotinus saw the ideas of things in the eternal mind, and unfolded all mysteries with the Schoolmen and fathomed the depths of Duns Scotus and Thomas Aquinas, and entered the third heaven with Jacob Behmen, and walked hand in hand with Swedenborg through the pavilions of the New Jerusalem, and sung his faith in the promise and in the word in his *Religious Musings*—and lowering himself from that dizzy height, poised himself on Milton's wings, and spread out his thoughts in charity with the glad prose of Jeremy Taylor, and wept over Bowles's Sonnets, and studied Cowper's blank verse, and betook himself to Thomson's Castle of Indolence, and sported with the wits of Charles the Second's days and of Queen Anne, and relished Swift's style and that of the John Bull (Arbuthnot's we mean, not Mr Croker's), and dallied with the British Essayists and Novelists, and knew all qualities of more modern writers with a learned spirit, Johnson, and Goldsmith, and Junius, and Burke, and Godwin, and the Sorrows of Werter, and Jean Jacques Rousseau, and Voltaire, and Marivaux, and Crebillon, and thousands more—now 'laughed with Rabelais in his easy chair' or pointed to Hogarth, or afterwards dwelt on Claude's classic scenes, or spoke with rapture of Raphael, and compared the women at Rome to figures that had walked out of his pictures, or visited the Oratory of Pisa, and described the works of Giotto and Ghirlandaio and Massaccio, and gave the moral of the picture of the Triumph of Death, where the beggars and the wretched invoke his dreadful dart, but the rich and mighty of the earth quail and shrink before it; and in that land of siren sights and sounds, saw a dance of peasant girls, and was charmed with lutes and gondolas,—or wandered into Germany and lost himself in the labyrinths of the Hartz Forest and of the Kantean philosophy, and amongst the cabalistic names of Fichte and Schelling and Lessing, and God knows who—this was long after, but all the former while, he had nerved his heart and filled his eyes with tears, as he hailed the rising orb of liberty, since quenched in darkness and in blood, and had kindled his affections at the blaze of the French Revolution, and sang for joy when the towers of the Bastile and the proud places of the insolent and the oppressor fell, and would have floated his bark, freighted with fondest fancies, across the Atlantic wave with Southey and others to seek for peace and freedom—

In Philarmonia's undivided dale![68]

At the end of this mighty sentence, outside and as a new paragraph, comes the sting:

Alas! 'Frailty, thy name is *Genius!*'—What is become of all this mighty heap of hope, of thought, of learning, and humanity? It has ended in swallowing doses of oblivion, and in writing paragraphs in the *Courier.*—Such, and so little is the mind of man![69]

The virtuoso expansion of the one-sentence intellectual biography is rhetorically justified by the marvellous anti-climax of the conclusion: 'It has ended in swallowing doses of oblivion and in writing paragraphs in the *Courier.*' But the passage is more than a triumph of rhetoric; it is also an incontrovertible witness to Hazlitt's almost overwhelmed sense of Coleridge's powers; even phrases such as 'this mighty heap of hope, of thought, of learning, and of humanity', despite the denigrative uses to which they are put, testify to an observer profoundly impressed, awed, rather, by the figure of Coleridge.

That awe might not be readily apparent in the most scathing of Hazlitt's criticisms of Coleridge, those, say, of his *Lay Sermons* and of his *Biographia Literaria,* but even in those acid pieces careful reading reveals its presence.[70] Elsewhere, it is unmistakable:

Hardly a speculation has been left on record from the earliest time, but it is loosely folded up in Mr Coleridge's memory, like a rich, but somewhat tattered piece of tapestry: we might add (with more seeming than real extravagance), that scarce a thought can pass through the mind of man, but its sound has at some time or other passed over his head with rustling pinions. On whatever question or author you speak, he is prepared to take up the theme with advantage—from

---

[68] Ibid. 32–4.   [69] Ibid. 34.

[70] For a single instance, even in the acidulous mock-review written prior to the appearance of the first *Lay Sermon,* Hazlitt says: 'Let him talk on for ever in this world and the next; and both worlds will be the better for it. But let him not write, or pretend to write, nonsense. Nobody is the better for it.' (*Hazlitt,* vii. 118). Cf. E.K. Chambers: 'Then in September came, also in *The Examiner,* a very definite act of hostility to Coleridge, also in the form of a review, but a bogus one, of what Hazlitt felt sure that Coleridge would write in his *Lay Sermon,* then already announced, but not yet published. It was a masterpiece of malicious irony. Both Lamb and Robinson were perturbed, although Lamb acutely observed that after all "a kind of respect shines thro' the disrespect". This, indeed, is the case with nearly all of Hazlitt's writings upon Coleridge' (Chambers, 296).

Peter Abelard down to Thomas Moore. . . . There is no man of genius, in whose praise he descants, but the critic seems to stand above the author . . . nor is there any work of genius that does not come out of his hands like an illuminated Missal, sparkling even in its defects.[71]

Hazlitt was so profoundly impressed, indeed, that it was necessary to react to Coleridge all the more adversely in order, in Bloom's formula, 'to clear imaginative space' for himself. Coleridge's admirers frequently found themselves disappointed, but none was so disappointed as Hazlitt, and in the depth and varied repetition of that disappointment we see the shape of the weapon Hazlitt found it necessary to use to free himself from Coleridge.

For in certain respects, not merely those of their extraordinarily keen critical perceptions, they were much alike. Both were the sons of preachers. Hazlitt's father seems to have been more forceful than Coleridge's, and the son's relationship to the father more satisfactory also ('His father's piety, his integrity, and his benign confidence in the triumph of reform stayed in Hazlitt's memory', notes Herschel Baker, who sees in Hazlitt's background of religious dissent a significant formative influence on his subsequent thought).[72] Both Hazlitt and Coleridge were deeply committed to philosophy. Even when Hazlitt dismisses Coleridge's *Friend* with contempt, the gesture is reflexive: 'What is his *Friend* itself but an enormous title-page; the longest and most tiresome prospectus that ever was written; an endless preface to an imaginary work; a table of contents that fills the whole volume; a huge bill of fare of all possible subjects, with not an idea to be had for love or money.'[73] Yet Hazlitt too had indulged in an unfulfilled prospectus. An eight-page pamphlet published in 1809 bore the title 'Proposals for Publishing, in One Large Volume, Quarto (price 1*l.* 10*s.* to Subscribers), A HISTORY OF ENGLISH PHILOSOPHY . . . '.[74]

Thirdly, both Hazlitt and Coleridge were deeply committed to political observation and theory. Indeed, a fine example of how close they at times could be, despite Hazlitt's later rage over what he considered Coleridge's apostasy from the libertarian faith, was their attitude towards Pitt. Each produced portraits of the British statesman, and it is instructive to compare portions of two of them in matters of style and emphasis. First Coleridge:

---

[71] *Hazlitt*, xi. 29–30.
[72] Herschel Baker, *William Hazlitt* (Cambridge, Mass.: Harvard University Press, 1962), 21.   [73] *Hazlitt*, vii. 115.   [74] Ibid. ii. 112.

William Pitt was the younger son of Lord Chatham; a fact of no ordinary importance in the solution of his character, of no mean significance in the heraldry of morals and intellect. His father's rank, fame, political connections, and parental ambition were his mould;—he was cast, rather than grew. A palpable election, a conscious predestination controlled the free agency, and transfigured the individuality of his mind; and that, which he *might have been*, was compelled into that, which he *was to be*. From his early childhood it was his father's custom to make him stand up on a chair and declaim before a large company; by which exercise, practised so frequently, and continued for so many years, he acquired a premature and unnatural dexterity in the combination of words, which must of necessity have diverted his attention from present objects, obscured his impressions, and deadened his genuine feelings. Not the *thing* on which he was speaking, but the praises to be gained by the speech, were present to his intuition; hence he associated all the operations of his faculties with words, and his pleasures with the surprise excited by them. . . . The young Pitt was conspicuous far beyond his fellows, both at school and at college. He was always full grown: he had neither the promise nor the awkwardness of growing intellect. Vanity, early satiated, formed and elevated itself into a love of power; and in losing this colloquial vanity he lost one of the prime links that connect the individual with the species, too early for the affections, though not too early for the understanding.[75]

The virtuoso analysis by Coleridge is properly juxtaposed against a virtuoso analysis by Hazlitt:

The character of Mr Pitt was, perhaps, one of the most singular that ever existed. With few talents, and fewer virtues, he acquired and preserved in one of the most trying situations, and in spite of all opposition, the highest reputation for the possession of every moral excellence, and as having carried the attainments of eloquence and wisdom as far as human abilities could go. This he did (strange as it appears) by a negation (together with the common virtues) of the common vices of human nature, and by the complete negation of every other talent that might interfere with the only one which he possessed in a supreme degree, and which indeed may be made to include the appearance of others—an artful use of words, and a certain dexterity of logical arrangement. In these alone his power consisted. . . . Having no strong feelings, no distinct perceptions, his mind having no link, as it were, to connect it with the world of external nature, every subject presented to him nothing more than a *tabula rasa*, on which he was at liberty to lay whatever colouring of language he pleased; having no general principles, no comprehensive views of things, no moral habits of thinking, no system of action, there was nothing to hinder him from pursuing any particular purpose, by any means that offered; having never any plan, he could not be convicted of inconsistency, and his own pride and obstinacy were the only rules

[75] *Inquiring Spirit: A New Presentation of Coleridge from his Published and Unpublished Prose Writings*, ed. Kathleen Coburn (New York: Pantheon Books, 1951), 269.

of his conduct. Having no insight into human nature, no sympathy with the passions of men, or apprehension of their real designs, he seemed perfectly insensible to the consequences of things, and would believe nothing till it actually happened. The fog and haze in which he saw every thing communicated itself to others; and the total indistinctness and uncertainty of his own ideas tended to confound the perceptions of his hearers more effectually than the most ingenious misrepresentation could have done.[76]

The savage parallelisms of Hazlitt's analysis serve to discredit Pitt by presenting him as cut off from the common experience of mankind; the equal devastation of Coleridge's analysis does this too and is further achieved by a utilization of the principle of organic form to describe the deficiencies of Pitt's growth.

But Hazlitt's initial admiration of Coleridge gave way to disappointment, and it was disappointment of a particular intensity. For this was the condition by which Hazlitt could attain intellectual adulthood. Indeed, even the episode, disgraceful by the mores of the time even if almost ludicrous by ours,[77] by which Hazlitt came into the permanent moralistic disapproval of Wordsworth and Coleridge, served the purposes of his larger development, despite the personal pain and humiliation he no doubt experienced. The story became embellished by repeated retelling, but Crabb Robinson probably reports its substance more or less correctly:

It appears that Hazlitt, when at Keswick, narrowly escaped being ducked by the populace, and probably sent to prison for some gross attacks on women. (He even whipped one woman, *more puerorum*, for not yielding to his wishes.) The populace were incensed against him and pursued him, but he escaped to Wordsworth, who took him into his house at midnight, gave him clothes and money (from three to five pounds). Since that time Wordsworth, though he never refused to meet Hazlitt when by accident they came together, did not choose that with his knowledge he should be invited.[78]

---

[76] *Hazlitt*, vii. 322–3.

[77] But Lamb, too, thought the episode more comic than disgraceful. As he writes to Wordsworth about the event: 'The "scapes" of the great god Pan who appeared among your mountains some dozen years since, and his narrow chance of being submerged by the swains, afforded me much pleasure. I can conceive the water nymphs pulling for him' (Lamb, *Letters*, iii. 125. 28 Dec. 1814).

[78] *Robinson*, i. 169–70. 15 June 1815. Patmore speaks of 'Hazlitt's alleged treatment of some pretty village jilt, who, when he was on a visit to Wordsworth, had led him (Hazlitt) to believe that she was not insensible to his attentions; and then, having induced him to "commit" himself to her in some ridiculous manner, turned round upon him, and made him the laughing-stock of the village. . . . And his conduct on this occasion is understood to have been the immediate cause of that breach between him and his friends above-named (at least Wordsworth and Southey), which was never afterwards healed' (Patmore, iii. 141–2).

Some twenty years after the event, in 1824, Wordsworth told the painter Benjamin Robert Haydon about Hazlitt's 'licentious conduct', that 'No woman could walk after dark, for "his Satyr & *beastly* appetites."' He went on to say that 'some girl called him a black-faced rascal, when Hazlitt enraged pushed her down, "& because, Sir," said Wordsworth, "she refused to gratify his abominable & devilish propensities," he lifted up her petticoats "& *smote* her on the *bottom*".'[79]

Coleridge was hardly less disapproving than Wordsworth, and in fact usually invoked the episode with a tone almost of hysteria.[80] In 1816 he wrote to Hugh Rose and spoke of 'William Hazlitt, whom I befriended for several years with the most improvident kindness when he was utterly friendless—and whom Southey and myself at our own hazard saved from infamy and transportation in return for his having done his best by the most loathsome conduct . . . to bring disgrace on our names and families.'[81] To be sure, Hazlitt had just then written a very severe review of Coleridge's *Statesman's Manual* for the *Examiner*, and as he continued to write scathing articles about his former idol, Coleridge in 1817 turned up his own rhetoric to higher pitch:

. . . the author of the Articles in the Edingburgh Review, and the Examiner (W. Hazlitt) after efforts of friendship on my part which a Brother could not have demanded, my House, Purse, Influence—& all this, tho' his manners were dreadfully repulsive to me, because I was persuaded that he was a young man of great Talent and utterly friendless—his very Father & Mother having despaired of him . . . after having been snatched from an infamous Punishment by Southey and myself (there were not less than 200 men on horse in search of him)—after having given him all the money, I had in the world, and the very Shoes off my feet to enable him to escape over the mountains—and since that time never, either of us, injured him in the least degree—unless the quiet withdrawing from any further connection with him . . .—not merely or chiefly on account of his Keswick Conduct, but from the continued depravity of his Life—but why need I say more?—This man Mr Jeffery has sought out, knowing all this, because the wretch is notorious for his avowed Hatred to *me*. . . . He has repeatedly boasted, that he wrote the very contrary of all, he believed—because he was under heavy obligations, and therefore *hated* me.[82]

Coleridge, his indignation notwithstanding, may have rather shrewdly hit the mark: it was psychologically necessary for Hazlitt to turn against Coleridge in order to become his own man intellectually; and the coarctive imagination served to make adverse occasions more

[79] *Haydon*, ii. 470.   [80] For extended discussion see Chambers, 295–9.
[81] Coleridge, *Letters*, iv. 669–70. 17 Sept. 1816.   [82] Ibid. 735–6. 5 June 1817.

extreme. Also, there is corroborative indication that Coleridge did find Hazlitt's manners repellent and did disapprove of his womanizing even before the scandal, and before the two great critics came to a parting of the ways. Thus on 16 September 1803, Coleridge wrote to Thomas Wedgwood in memorable terms about the young painter:

William Hazlitt is a thinking, observant, original man. . . . His manners are to 99 in 100 singularly repulsive—: brow-hanging, shoe-contemplative, *strange*. . . . [H]e is, I verily believe, kindly-natured—is very fond of, attentive to, & patient with, children / but he is jealous, gloomy, & of an irritable Pride—& addicted to women, as objects of sexual Indulgence. With all this, there is much good in him—he is disinterested, an enthusiastic Lover of the great men, who have been before us—he says things that are his own in a way of his own. . . . He sends well-headed & well-feathered Thoughts straight forwards to the mark with a Twang of the Bow-string.[83]

Coleridge was characteristically acute in his assessment of Hazlitt's abilities; he was not overwhelmed, however, as Hazlitt was in return. Thinking back to his first meeting with Coleridge in 1798, Hazlitt says: 'a sound was in my ears as of a Siren's song; I was stunned, startled with it as from deep sleep; but I had no notion that I should ever be able to express my admiration to others in motley imagery or quaint allusion till the light of [Coleridge's] genius shone into my soul.'[84] He continues:

I was at that time dumb, inarticulate, helpless, like a worm by the way-side, crushed, bleeding, lifeless; but now, bursting from the deadly bands that 'bound them,

'With Styx nine times round them,'

my ideas float on winged words, and as they expand their plumes, catch the golden light of other years. My soul has indeed remained in its original bondage, dark, obscure, with longings infinite and unsatisfied; my heart, shut up in the prison-house of this rude clay, has never found, nor will it ever find, a heart to speak to; but that my understanding also did not remain dumb and brutish, or at length found a language to express itself, I owe to Coleridge.[85]

Throughout this extended reminiscence, which is called 'My First Acquaintance With Poets', Hazlitt sets the bedazzled parameters in which all his subsequent ferocious criticism of Coleridge must be seen:

It was in January, 1798, that I rose one morning before daylight, to walk ten miles in the mud, and went to hear this celebrated person preach. Never the longest day I have to live, shall I have such another walk as this cold, raw,

---

[83]Ibid. ii. 990–1.   [84]*Hazlitt*, xvii. 107.   [85]Ibid.

comfortless one, in the winter of the year 1798. . . . When I got there, the organ was playing the 100th psalm, and, when it was done, Mr Coleridge rose and gave out his text, 'And he went up into the mountain to pray, HIMSELF, ALONE.' As he gave out his text, his voice 'rose like a steam of rich distilled perfumes,' and when he came to the two last words, which he pronounced loud, deep, and distinct, it seemed to me, who was then young, as if the sounds had echoed from the bottom of the human heart, and as if that prayer might have floated in solemn silence through the universe. . . . The preacher then launched into his subject, like an eagle dallying with the wind. The sermon was upon peace and war; upon church and state—not their alliance, but their separation—on the spirit of the world and the spirit of Christianity, not as the same, but as opposed to one another. . . . And for myself, I could not have been more delighted if I had heard the music of the spheres. Poetry and philosophy had met together. Truth and Genius had embraced, under the eye and with the sanction of Religion.[86]

This is almost rapturous. But closer acquaintance merely increased Hazlitt's thraldom. Burke, interestingly enough, was a prime link in the chain that early bound Hazlitt to Coleridge:

Coleridge seemed to take considerable notice of me, and that of itself was enough. . . . At dinner-time he grew more animated, and dilated in a very edifying manner on Mary Wollstonecraft and Mackintosh. The last, he said, he considered . . . a clever scholastic man . . . the ready warehouseman of letters, who knew exactly where to lay his hand on what he wanted, though the goods were not his own. He thought him no match for Burke, either in style or matter. Burke was a metaphysician, Mackintosh a mere logician. Burke was an orator (almost a poet) who reasoned in figures, because he had an eye for nature: Mackintosh, on the other hand, was a rhetorician, who had only an eye to common-places. On this I ventured to say that I had always entertained a great opinion of Burke, and that . . . the speaking of him with contempt might be made the test of a vulgar democratical mind. This was the first observation I ever made to Coleridge, and he said it was a very just and striking one. I remember the leg of Welsh mutton and the turnips on the table that day had the finest flavour imaginable. Coleridge added that Mackintosh and Tom Wedgwood (of whom, however, he spoke highly) had expressed a very indifferent opinion of his friend Mr Wordsworth, on which he remarked to them—'He strides on so far before you that he dwindles in the distance!'[87]

When the two men parted, it was to leave a thoroughly mesmerized Hazlitt:

On my way back, I had a sound in my ears, it was the voice of Fancy: I had a light before me, it was the face of Poetry. . . . I had an uneasy, pleasurable

[86] Ibid. 108.   [87] Ibid. 111.

sensation all the time, till I was to visit him. During those months the chill breath of winter gave me a welcoming; the vernal air was balm and inspiration to me. The golden sunsets, the silver star of evening, lighted me on my way to new hopes and prospects. *I was to visit Coleridge in the spring.* This circumstance was never absent from my thoughts, and mingled with all my feelings.[88]

Coleridge, who had never been mesmerized by Hazlitt in return, could hardly understand the depth of the latter's feelings of rejection after the sexual scandal.[89] He refers repeatedly to Hazlitt's 'rancorous Hatred',[90] and he tended to think Hazlitt's severe criticisms simply exercises in unprovoked malice. It seems humorous to us, though not at all so to Coleridge, that he believed that 'Hazlitt from pure malignity has spread about the Report that Geraldine was a man in disguise'.[91] The charge, however trivial, witnesses an irreducible aspect of Hazlitt's critical integrity, that even in vendetta he saw clearly; for the reference focuses for us what is of greatest moment in 'Christabel', although curiously unrecognized by Coleridge himself, that is, that the relation of Christabel and Geraldine is palpably sexual, even if we today think of it in lesbian rather than heterosexual terms. Speaking in another letter of 'Mr Hazlitt's frantic hatred toward me', Coleridge says that Hazlitt 'set about the report, that the GERALDINE in my Christabel was a man in disguise, and that the whole Poem had an obscene purpose'.[92]

What actually interested Hazlitt most about 'Christabel', however, was not its intense current of sexuality, but its recognition of lost friendship. Thus in his *Lectures on the English Poets* he writes of Coleridge (and he points to the passage on other occasions as well):

There is one fine passage in his Christabel, that which contains the description of the quarrel between Sir Leoline and Sir Roland de Vaux of Tryermaine, who had been friends in youth.

[88] Ibid. 115.

[89] Even the not very perceptive Haydon understood matters more clearly: '. . . when he heard Wordsworth was coming to town, he wrote a fine puffing criticism on the Excursion, in hopes of preparing the way for a reconciliation. Wordsworth's utter contempt for his character induced him to take no notice whatever of this piece of petty finesse. Hazlitt now became amazed, & stung at Wordsworth's neglect, thundered forth those attacks on the whole Lake School . . .' (*Haydon*, ii. 494–5). As Robinson notes, 'Lamb . . . rather reproaches Wordsworth for being inveterate against Hazlitt' (*Robinson*, i. 170).

[90] e.g., Coleridge, *Letters*, iv. 813. 17 Jan. 1818.

[91] Ibid. 918. 31 Jan. 1819.

[92] Ibid. 9 Feb. 1819. See further John Beer, 'Coleridge, Hazlitt, and "Christabel"', *Review of English Studies*, NS, 37 (Feb. 1986), 40–54.

> Alas! they had been friends in youth
> But whispering tongues can poison truth;
> And constancy lives in realms above;
> And life is thorny, and youth is vain;
> And to be wroth with one we love,
> Doth work like madness in the brain;
>
> .　　.　　.　　.　　.　　.
>
> They stood aloof, the scars remaining,
> Like cliffs which had been rent asunder;
> A dreary sea now flows between,
> But neither heat, nor frost, nor thunder,
> Shall wholly do away I ween
> The marks of that which once hath been.[93]

Indeed, when he thinks of broken friendship, Hazlitt's controlled pessimism can become something much more bitter. As he rather startlingly says in an essay called 'On the Pleasure of Hating':

I was taught to think, and I was willing to believe, that genius was not a bawd—that virtue was not a mask—that liberty was not a name—that love had its seat in the human heart. Now I would care little if these words were struck out of the dictionary, or if I had never heard them. They are become to my ears a mockery and a dream. . . . Seeing all this as I do, and unravelling the web of human life into its various threads of meanness, spite, cowardice, want of feeling, and want of understanding, of indifference towards others and ignorance of ourselves—seeing custom prevail over all excellence, itself giving way to infamy—mistaken as I have been in my public and private hopes, calculating others from myself, and calculating wrong; always disappointed where I placed most reliance; the dupe of friendship, and the fool of love; have I not reason to hate and despise myself? Indeed, I do; and chiefly for not having hated and despised the world enough.[94]

The snarl at the end of the passage is less impressive than the scathing catalogue that precedes it. As 'the dupe of friendship, and the fool of love', Hazlitt could indeed feel disappointed. His obsession for Sarah Walker ravaged him—to find a parallel we perhaps have to go to the devastated hopes for Albertine recorded in Proust's novel—and one can hardly exaggerate the torment and disappointment he suffered:[95]

---

[93] *Hazlitt*, v. 166.　　　[94] Ibid. xii. 135–6.

[95] As Hazlitt wrote to Patmore: 'What have I suffered since I parted with you! A raging fire in my heart and in my brain, that I thought would drive me mad. . . . The abyss was before me, and *her* face, where all my peace was centred—all lost! I felt the eternity of punishment in this world. Mocked, mocked by her in whom I placed my hope—writhing, withering in misery and despair, caused by one who hardens herself against me. I wished

My heart is torn out of me, and every feeling for which I wished to live. It is like a dream, an enchantment; it torments me and it makes me mad. I lie down with it, I rise up with it, and I see no chance of repose, I grasp at a shadow, I try to undo the past, or to make that mockery real, and I weep with rage and pity over my own weakness and misery. . . . I am in some sense proud that I can feel this dreadful passion—it makes me a kind of peer in the kingdom of love, but I could have wished it had been for an object that at least could have understood its value and pitied its excess.[96]

To be equated with this torment, the disappointment with Coleridge had to be profound indeed.

It was. Though disappointment with Coleridge took pride of place with Hazlitt's dashed hopes for political reform and with the frustrations of his heart's passions, his cynicism towards and censure of Coleridge's failure could never erase the substratum of awestruck admiration that Coleridge first, last, and always aroused in him. In the following passage, what begins as enormous compliment turns immediately to contemptuous dismissal, then rises again to a paean of praise and wonder before subsiding again into disappointment. The effect is of a kind of recapitulation of Hazlitt's entire involvement with Coleridge:

The man of perhaps the greatest ability now living is the one who has not only done the least, but who is actually incapable of ever doing any thing worthy of him—unless he had a hundred hands to write with, and a hundred mouths to utter all that it hath entered into his heart to conceive, and centuries before him to embody the endless volume of his waking dreams. Cloud rolls over cloud; one train of thought suggests and is driven away by another; theory after theory is spun out of the bowels of his brain. . . . No subject can come amiss to him . . . his mind every where finding its level, and feeling no limit but that of thought . . . passing from Duns Scotus to Jacob Behmen, from the Kantean philosophy to a conundrum, and from the Apocalypse to an acrostic—taking in the whole range of poetry, painting, wit, history, politics, metaphysics, criticism, and private

---

for courage to throw myself into the waters; but I could not even do that—and my little boy, too, prevented me, when I thought of his face at hearing of his father's death, and his desolation in life' (Patmore, iii. 176). De Quincey, with uncommon sympathy and insight, defended Hazlitt's publication of his lover's anguish: '. . . people generally, who could not be aware of his feelings, or the way in which this treachery acted upon his mind as a ratification of all the other wrongs that he had suffered through life, laughed at him, or expressed disgust for him as too coarsely indelicate in making such disclosures. But there was no indelicacy in such an act of confidence,—growing, as it did, out of his lacerated heart. It was an explosion of frenzy. He threw out his clamorous anguish to the winds, and to the air, caring not *who* might listen, *who* might sympathise, or who might sneer. Pity was no demand of his; laughter was no wrong; the sole necessity for *him* was to empty his over-burdened spirit' (*De Quincey*, xi. 346).   [96] Hazlitt, *Letters*, 275. 28 June 1822.

scandal—every question giving birth to some new thought, and every thought
'discoursed in eloquent music', that lives only in the ear of fools, or in the report
of absent friends. Set him to write a book, and he belies all that has been ever
said about him—

> Ten thousand great ideas filled his mind,
> But with the clouds they fled, and left no trace behind.[97]

Yet they left behind, indelibly, traces, permanent and definitive, in
Hazlitt's own mind. A fitting quotation with which to conclude, and,
alas, to truncate this discussion of the most intense and complex
intellectual relationship of his life is a sudden and unanticipated
confession that Hazlitt makes at the end of his *Lectures on the English
Poets*. After severe and dismissive comments on Coleridge—he has
just said that 'His *Conciones ad Populum*, Watchman, &c. are dreary
trash'—Hazlitt concludes, as this chapter shall also, with these intense
words:

But I may say of him here, that he is the only person I ever knew who answered to
the idea of a man of genius. He is the only person from whom I ever learnt any
thing. There is only one thing he could learn from me in return, but *that* he has
not. He was the first poet I ever knew. His genius at that time had angelic wings,
and fed on manna. He talked on for ever; and you wished him to talk on for ever.
His thoughts did not seem to come with labour and effort; but as if borne on the
gusts of genius. . . . His voice rolled on the ear like the pealing organ. . . . His
mind was clothed with wings; and raised on them, he lifted philosophy to
heaven. In his descriptions, you then saw the progress of human happiness and
liberty in bright and never-ending succession, like the steps of Jacob's ladder . . .
and with the voice of God at the top of the ladder. And shall I, who heard him
then, listen to him now? Not I! . . . That spell is broke; that time is gone for ever;
that voice is heard no more; but still the recollection comes rushing by with
thoughts of long-past years, and rings in my ears with never-dying sound.[98]

With this climax Hazlitt does not let well enough alone, but characteristically misfocuses his style by appending an appositional quotation, or
rather misquotation:

> What though the radiance which was once so bright,
> Be now for ever taken from my sight,
> Though nothing can bring back the hour
> Of glory in the grass, of splendour in the flow'r;
>   I do not grieve, but rather find
>   Strength in what remains behind;

[97] *Hazlitt*, xii. 198–9.   [98] Ibid. v. 167.

And he continues the quotation down through the words,

> In years that bring the philosophic mind![99]

But then the realization dawns upon us that it is fitting that we see both sides of Hazlitt's coarctive imagination in a moment of such intensity, and we realize further that for once the disparate areas of his concern coincide as a witness to the integrated truth of his feeling and thought.

For Coleridge, and the loss of Coleridge, the inspiration afforded by Coleridge, and the disappointment occasioned by Coleridge, were the deepest and most constant themes, frequently expressed, more often subliminal, of Hazlitt's entire intellectual career.

[99] Ibid. 167–8.

4
De Quincey's Journey to the End of Night

IT is De Quincey, among the great trio of early nineteenth-century English essayists, who stands least obscured in traditional perspectives on Romanticism.[1] In large part this is because his most widely disseminated work, *The Confessions of an English Opium-Eater*, takes up and passes on themes recognized as central to any conception of an inner essence for the Romantic movement. The intent and reverberation of the word 'confessions' latch on the founding figure, Rousseau, and they also convey those overtones of egotism and sickness that Babbitt, in his *Rousseau and Romanticism*, finds normative for Romanticism as a whole. In the figure of Werther no less than that of Chateaubriand's René, self-preoccupation and inner sickness early found fictional co-ordinates, and De Quincey's self-presentation as the Opium-Eater is semi-fictional no less than Rousseauistically autobiographical.

In being not only a 'confessions', but also the revelations of an opium addict, De Quincey's work doubles its Romantic credentials, so to speak, for as documented in Alethea Hayter's *Opium and the Romantic Imagination*, not to mention more specialized treatises like Molly LeFebure's *Samuel Taylor Coleridge: A Bondage of Opium* or Elisabeth Schneider's *Coleridge, Opium, and 'Kubla Khan'*, drugs were a major criterion of Romanticism, not alone as pathological symptom (Romanticism, in Goethe's famous definition, is 'the sick'), but as imaginative source as well. Here De Quincey is the most pivotal figure of all. Not only is it he who makes new literary capital of a theme that Coleridge perhaps knew more about, and certainly knew earlier, but he it was also who handed the drug motif to French Romanticism. Alfred de Musset translated De Quincey's *Confessions of an English Opium-Eater* into French in 1828. More significantly, Baudelaire, after thinking about the matter for a decade and longer, in 1860 published a treatise called *Les Paradis artificiels*, which bears the subtitle 'On wine and hashish, compared as a means of expanding individuality'. Baudelaire

[1] For instance, V. A. De Luca's *Thomas De Quincey: The Prose of Vision* (Toronto: University of Toronto Press, 1980), contains an 'Epilogue' entitled 'De Quincey's Place in the Romantic Tradition', 147–50.

called the last section *Un Mangeur d'opium*, and it consists of mingled translation from, and summary and discussion of, De Quincey's masterpiece. De Quincey, in truth, much more than either Lamb or Hazlitt, has been an influence on later writers outside the borders of England. In our own century Jorge Luis Borges has spoken eloquently of his fascination with De Quincey, and there seems to be a definite stylistic succession running from De Quincey to Proust by way of Pater and Ruskin.

But it is not merely in its structure as confession and its apotheosis of drugs, nor even in its influence, that the *Confessions of an English Opium-Eater* (the modifying specification, 'English', almost guaranteed continental attention) is central to Romanticism. In its tone and inner detail, too, it is quintessentially Romantic. For here are presented archetypal loci both of dream and of oriental reference, two of the major criteria of Romanticism as enumerated in the first chapter of this volume. Both criteria are interwoven in a single fabric. Indeed, 'the main subject' of the latter part of the *Confessions* is 'the history and journal of what took place in my dreams':

Under the connecting feeling of tropical heat and vertical sunlights I brought together all creatures, birds, beasts, reptiles, all trees and plants, usages and appearances that are found in all tropical regions, and assembled them together in China or Indostan. From kindred feelings I soon brought Egypt and all her gods under the same law. I was stared at, hooted at, grinned at, chattered at by monkeys, by parrakeets, by cockatoos. I ran into pagodas and was fixed for centuries at the summit or in secret rooms; I was the idol; I was the priest; I was worshipped; I was sacrificed. I fled from the wrath of Brahma through all the forests of Asia; Vishnu hated me; Siva laid wait for me. I came suddenly upon Isis and Osiris; I had done a deed, they said, which the ibis and the crocodile trembled at. I was buried, for a thousand years, in stone coffins, with mummies and sphinxes, in narrow chambers at the heart of eternal pyramids. I was kissed, with cancerous kisses, by crocodiles and laid, confounded with all unutterable slimy things, amongst reeds and Nilotic mud.

I thus give the reader some slight abstraction of my Oriental dreams, which always filled me with such amazement at the monstrous scenery that horror seemed absorbed, for a while, in sheer astonishment.[2]

Despite his central position in Romanticism, however, and notwith-

---

[2] De Quincey, *Confessions*, 95–6. Cf. Baudelaire: 'The ability to dream is divine and mysterious by nature; for it is through dream that man communicates with the obscure and unknown world that surrounds him. But this ability requires solitude for its free development; the more a man withdraws within himself, the more apt he is to dream richly, deeply. Now, what solitude could be greater, calmer, more remote from the sphere of worldly concerns, than the solitude that opium creates?' (*Baudelaire*, i. 497).

standing his international influence, De Quincey is a figure who seems
never to have been taken entirely seriously, either by later critics or by
his own contemporaries. Everyone loved Lamb, even Hazlitt did,[3] and
almost everyone except Lamb and of course Keats gave the morose and
lethal Hazlitt a wide berth.[4] 'Hazlitt', said De Quincey, 'smiled on no
man, nor exchanged tokens of peace with the nearest of fraternities.'
'*Whatever is*—so much I conceive to have been a fundamental lemma for
Hazlitt—*is wrong.*' 'Hazlitt viewed all personal affronts or casual slights
towards himself as tending to something more general. . . . It was not
Hazlitt whom the wretches struck at; no, no; it was democracy, or it was
freedom, or it was Napoleon, whose shadow they saw in the rear of
Hazlitt. . . .'[5] No one, however, gave De Quincey a wide berth; rather,
people tended scarcely to notice him. A suggestive anecdote is supplied
by De Quincey himself. Trying to persuade the mentally disturbed
Charles Lloyd that Lloyd was not, as he declared himself to be, the
Devil, De Quincey was taken aback by Lloyd's rejoinder: 'I know who
you are; you are nobody, a nonentity; you have no being. . . . You will
attempt to argue with me, and thus to prove that you do exist; but it is not
so, you do not exist at all.'[6]

It was not only his amiable manners and an almost tail-wagging
gentleness that worked against De Quincey's being taken seriously; it
was even more, and almost tragically, that he was so physically minute.
Keats, who was also small, overheard someone say that he was 'quite the
little Poet', and commented, 'now this is abominable—you might as well
say Buonaparte is quite the little Soldier—You see what it is to be under

---

[3] As Patmore recalls, 'Hazlitt felt towards Lamb a sentiment of personal kindness and
esteem that was not extended, even in kind, to any other individual' (Patmore, ii. 330).

[4] e.g. Robinson: 'Returned to Lamb's. Hazlitt was there, and overbearing and rude. . . .
He mixes passion and ill-humour and personal feelings in his judgments on public events
and characters more than any man I know . . .' (*Robinson*, i. 133). 'Hazlitt delights in
bidding defiance to common opinion, and there is a twist about either his head or heart'
(ibid. 151). '. . . his political and personal antipathies peep out very unpleasantly every
moment' (ibid. 226). 'Brown related anecdotes of Hazlitt's personal cowardice, as well as
of his slovenliness, and says he was the worst-tempered man he ever knew' (ibid. 387). Cf.
Haydon: 'Here's a man whom my generosity saved from starving . . . whose necessities I
have again and again assisted, to my own ruin . . . but whose heart is so innately fiendish,
nothing can soften or tame him. . . . He is disappointed in Politicks, disappointed in Art,
always in the wrong. . . . The keen malignity with which he has set his talents to weaken the
disposition now budding for English Art is extraordinary' (*Haydon*, ii. 495–6).

[5] *De Quincey*, xi. 342, 343–4. Speaking of 'the look of an incarnate demon's' that
sometimes crossed Hazlitt's face, Patmore says that 'it was almost always connected with
one of three topics—the downfall of Napoleon—the abuse of some deserving writer from
party motives—and (in the case where females were present) in reference to the passion of
Love' (Patmore, iii. 76).   [6] Lindop, 217.

six foot and not a lord.'[7] As Christopher Ricks has urged, 'there can be no doubt that Keats felt very strongly about his height (5 feet ¾ in.), and that this mattered most to him, and was an embarrassment more than superficial. . . . His poem "Had I a man's fair form" was glossed by his friend Woodhouse: "the author has an idea that the diminutiveness of his size makes him contemptible and that no woman can like a man of small stature." '[8]

De Quincey, though it is hard to believe, was even tinier than Keats. Leaving aside the personal embarrassments his stature undoubtedly generated for him, it caused others not to see the heroic dimension in his dark voyage through life.[9] None of the three great essayists could be said to be a very happy man, but Lamb notoriously stayed in place, while Hazlitt, though dragged around the northern United States as a child, and an eager visitor in Paris, retired early to his London lairs like a wounded animal.[10] De Quincey quotes from George Gilfillan's portrait of Hazlitt: 'With no hope, no fortune, no *status* in society, no certain popularity as a writer, no domestic peace, little sympathy from kindred spirits, little support from his political party, no moral management, no definite belief,—with great powers and great passions within, and with a host of powerful enemies without,—it was his to enact one of the saddest tragedies on which the sun ever shone.'[11] But Hazlitt, though unhappy, was known to be unhappy and in a sense respected for it. He could be seen as embodying the kind of heroism that at that time had received archetypal definition in the various heroes projected by Lord Byron.[12]

[7] Keats, *Letters*, ii. 61. 15 Feb. 1819.

[8] Christopher Ricks, *Keats and Embarrassment* (Oxford: Clarendon Press, 1974), 33–4.

[9] For instance, Dorothy Wordsworth writes of him in 1807: 'He is a remarkable and very interesting young man; very diminutive in person, which, to strangers, makes him appear insignificant' (*Middle Years*, i. 180). Cf. Carlyle: 'One of the smallest man figures I ever saw; shaped like a pair of tongs, and hardly above five feet in all. When he sate, you would have taken him, by candlelight, for the beautifullest little child.' (Carlyle, *Reminiscences*, 127).

[10] '. . . he could not, under the actual condition and circumstances of his mind and temper, have existed for any length of time out of London, or some other great metropolis . . .' (Patmore, iii. 18).   [11] *De Quincey*, xi. 353.

[12] Patmore records his first sight of Hazlitt in terms consonant with the sorrows and depths of the Byronic hero: 'There he sat, his anxious and highly-intellectual face looking upon vacancy; pale and silent as a ghost; emaciated as an anatomy. . . . And this "poor creature" (as he used sometimes to call himself)—apparently with scarcely energy enough to grapple with an infant or face a shadow—was the launcher forth of winged words that could shake the hearts of princes and potentates, and make them tremble in their seats of power; this effigy of silence was the utterer of floods of indignant eloquence that could rouse the soul of apathy itself, and stir the blood like the sound of a trumpet' (Patmore, ii. 252).

The Byronic hero has also always experienced a dark passage through a devastating past, but he stands with heroic pride in the present. Thus Byron's Lara:

> Whate'er he be, 'twas not what he had been:
> That brow in furrow'd lines had fix'd at last,
> And spake of passions, but of passion past.
> The pride, but not the fire, of early days,
> Coldness of mien, and carelessness of praise;
> A high demeanour, and a glance that took
> Their thoughts from others by a single look;[13]

No one could dare ignore such a figure; his night journey gave an awesome elevation to his presence. Thus Byron's Corsair:

> Lone, wild, and strange, he stood alike exempt
> From all affection and from all contempt:
> His name could sadden and his acts surprise,
> But they that fear'd him dared not to despise.[14]

Such was the Byronic hero; such was Hazlitt. But De Quincey, whose journey through life was no less dark than theirs, could not be exempt either from affection or from contempt. We should keep Lara and the Corsair in mind, as well as Manfred, the Giaour, and Childe Harold, when we encounter Carlyle's description of De Quincey:

He is one of the smallest men you ever in your life beheld; but with a most gentle and sensible face, only that the teeth are destroyed by opium, and the little bit of an under lip projects like a shelf. He speaks with a slow sad and soft voice, in the *politest* manner I have almost ever witnessed; ... Poor little fellow! It might soften a very hard heart to see him so courteous, yet so weak and poor; retiring *home* with his two children to a miserable lodging-house, and writing all day for the King of Donkies, the Proprietor of the Saturday Post.[15]

A certain contempt seems to mingle with Carlyle's affection. His wife, Jane, had nothing but affection, but of a kind not tending to enlist De Quincey among heroic figures either: 'What wouldn't one give', she once said, 'to have him in a box, and take him out to talk!'[16]

And yet, though his diminutive size made De Quincey seem almost a gentle spaniel, those who know him more deeply through his life and his writings have tended, bizarre though it seems, to class him among the heroes of existence. Thus Grevel Lindop concludes his biography of De Quincey with the following paragraph:

[13] Byron, *Lara; A Tale*, Canto I, ll. 66–72.
[14] Byron, *The Corsair; A Tale*, Canto I, ll. 271–4. [15] Carlyle, *Letters*, iv. 291.
[16] Carlyle, *Reminiscences*, 127.

But it is as the 'Opium-Eater' that he will be remembered. For better or worse, De Quincey remains the type of the literary drug-taker, which is certainly as he desired. The remarkable thing is that opium did not conquer him as it has conquered so many others. The drug dominated his life, and yet it was the creative imagination that triumphed. . . . [H]e did not close his eyes or resign himself to defeat, and despite the follies, indignities and failures of his life our final impression is of a man both lovable and oddly heroic.[17]

Baudelaire conveys the same impression. Hearing, during the composition of *Les Paradis artificiels*, of De Quincey's death, he speaks of him as having 'one of the most original' minds in 'all of England, but also one of the most affable and generous natures that ever honored literary history'; and as he resumes his summary of De Quincey's career in the fourth section of *Un Mangeur d'opium*, he calls him 'our hero', and observes parenthetically but emphatically, 'certainly he deserves this title'.[18]

Horace Ainsworth Eaton, in his biography of De Quincey of 1936, goes even further:

He was responsive to the gentler sides of life; to sympathy with the weak and suffering; to love, especially in regard to women and children. But more striking was his indomitable will, which is, as it were, the hard kernel of his character; so that throughout his bitter struggles against hardships, poverty, ill-health, mental misery and anguish, loss of wife and children he never completely despaired; but with little short of heroism, kept on to the end unbroken. He was no weakling, in spite of his diminutive size. . . . On the contrary, he was self-contained, self-assured, even, in a sense, arrogant underneath his outward gentleness. His nature made him essentially solitary in the fastness of his own personality, aloof from men and the world; and with unquestioning reliance upon his own measure of values. He was fundamentally resistant to the blows of fate and the consequences of his own weakness and mistakes.[19]

The heroic sense of De Quincey's life, which rises above the blocking elements of his gentleness and diminutive size, is generated by the feeling that he, far more than either Lamb or Hazlitt, was on a pilgrimage through life. In De Quincey, one of the profoundest motifs of Romanticism, the quest, seems to define the very structure of his existence. It is perhaps no accident that his greatest work was the vast, but Romantically fragmentary autobiography of which *The Confessions of an English Opium-Eater* and the *Suspiria de Profundis* are parts. One of

---

[17] Lindop, 392.
[18] 'notre héros (certes, il mérite bien ce titre)' (*Baudelaire*, i. 472).
[19] Horace Ainsworth Eaton, *Thomas De Quincey: A Biography* (New York: Oxford University Press, 1936), 510.

Baudelaire's paragraphs about him begins with the typical and sugges-tive statement, 'Once again he begins a wandering existence'.[20] And the sense that his life was a quest, a dark voyage through undiscovered lands,[21] and De Quincey himself a hero or kind of knight errant, is almost hypnotically suggested by the style in which these parts of his odyssey are recounted. Baudelaire can scarcely contain his admiration for this style. At one point, in his description of De Quincey's voyage through existence, he says: 'Here the tone of the book reaches such ele-vation that I conceive it my duty to let De Quincey speak for himself.'[22] He then translates De Quincey's prose at long and loving length.

Long and loving length is the norm by which De Quincey tends to be quoted. Masson, after somewhat coolly noting that the 'famous passages of "dream-phantasy"' in the *Opium Confessions* sometimes 'fail . . . by a swooning of the power of clear and consecutive vision on a mere piling and excess of imagery and sound',[23] nevertheless concludes his volume on De Quincey in the English Men of Letters series by quoting, in its entirety, the 'Ladies of Sorrow' passage from the 'Levana and Our Ladies of Sorrow' section of the *Suspiria*, with the comment that 'This is prose-poetry; but it is more. It is a permanent addition to the mythology of the human race.'[24] Nor can Baudelaire resist the hypnotic spell of De Quincey's prose, for he too ceases talking and translates at length the sinuous prose of 'Levana and Our Ladies of Sorrow', and at another point he says, 'The following pages are too beautiful to abridge', and quotes at length there too.[25]

In the conception of Levana we see further validation of the special shape of De Quincey's life as heroic quest, for the hero who journeys through dark regions must have a lady who, though absent, is his ideal, as Dante had Beatrice; the heroic knight performs all his actions for the sake of, and towards the hope of, the feminine, as even Don Quixote did for Dulcinea. 'Oftentimes at Oxford I saw Levana in my dreams', writes De Quincey:

I knew her by her Roman symbols. Who is Levana? . . . [T]hat mysterious lady, who never revealed her face (except to me in dreams), but always acted by

---

[20] 'Sa vie errante recommence' (*Baudelaire*, i. 452).

[21] A dark voyage indeed, in Carlyle's prescient observation: 'you would have taken him . . . for the beautifullest little child; blue-eyed, sparkling face, had there not been a something, too, which said "*Eccovi*—this child has been in hell"' (Carlyle, *Reminiscences*, 127).　　　[22] *Baudelaire*, i. 468.

[23] David Masson, *De Quincey* (New York: Harper & Brothers, 1882), 192.

[24] Ibid. 198.　　　[25] *Baudelaire*, i. 484.

delegation, had her name from the Latin verb (as still it is the Italian verb) *levare*, to raise aloft.[26]

The delegations authorized by Levana, who may perhaps be described as the feminine ideal that his mother's coldness always kept at a distance from him, were not just the three ladies of sorrow, but De Quincey's sisters, his daughters, his wife, and the lost London girl Ann. 'Das Ewigweibliche/Zieht uns hinan', says Goethe in the concluding lines of *Faust*.[27] In no other Romantic figure does the 'eternal feminine' draw us further than in De Quincey's life and art.[28] Baudelaire, indeed, speaks cannily of De Quincey's 'discerning and *feminine* style',[29] and he notes that men who, like De Quincey, have been

reared by and among women are not quite like other men, even if one presupposes an equality of temperament or intellectual ability. In a manner of speaking, the lullabies of nurse-maids, the maternal caresses, the dainty ways of sisters . . . serve to transform the dough of the masculine character by kneading it. A man who, from birth, has been long bathed in the softness of woman . . . ends by contracting a certain tenderness of skin, a certain refinement of speech, a sort of androgyny. . . . In the end, what I really want to say is that an early taste for the world of women, for *mundi mulieris* . . . makes for superior intellects . . .[30]

De Quincey's ideal of the feminine, however, was not happy and boisterous, but melancholy and sighing, as was the style he developed in which to record that ideal. For his deepest experience of the feminine was the experience of loss.[31] His mother was eccentric, dominating, but somewhat rejecting, and the child De Quincey accordingly invested enormous love in his sisters. But the enormous love was early conditioned by death. When he was in his fifth year his grandmother died, and then his younger sister, Jane, died also. Two years later these early experiences of loss were formed into the leitmotif of his very existence by the death, shattering to him for ever after, of the sister he loved most,

---

[26] De Quincey, *Confessions*, 172.   [27] *Goethe*, v. 526.

[28] e.g.: 'And when I was told insultingly to cease "my girlish tears", that word "*girlish*" had no sting for me, except as a verbal echo to the one eternal thought of my heart—that a girl was the sweetest thing I, in my short life, had known, that a girl it was who had crowned the earth with beauty and had opened to my thirst fountains of pure celestial love . . .' (De Quincey, *Confessions*, 137).

[29] 'la manière pénétrante et *féminine* de l'auteur' (*Baudelaire*, i. 447).

[30] Ibid. 499.

[31] Even on his deathbed the pattern prevailed: ' "How do you feel Papa now?" "Pretty comfortable, but who is that is asking?" "Emily, don't you know me Papa? Your daughter Emily." "Oh my love I am so glad to see you. I was afraid you had left me" ' (*De Quincey at Work*, 42).

Elizabeth. He stole into her room to see the corpse, and the memory is
one of the wonders of English literature:

Entering, I closed the door so softly that, although it opened upon a hall which
ascended through all the stores, no echo ran along the silent walls. Then turning
round, I sought my sister's face. But the bed had been moved, and the back was
now turned. Nothing met my eyes but one large window wide open, through
which the sun of midsummer at noonday was showering down torrents of
splendour. The weather was dry, the sky was cloudless, the blue depths seemed
the express types of infinity; and it was not possible for eye to behold or for heart
to conceive any symbols more pathetic of life and the glory of life. . . . From the
gorgeous sunlight I turned round to the corpse. There lay the sweet childish
figure, there the angel face. . . . I stood checked for a moment; awe, not fear, fell
upon me; and whilst I stood, a solemn wind began to blow—the most mournful
that ear ever heard. Mournful! That is saying nothing. It was a wind that had
swept the fields of mortality for a hundred centuries. Many times since, upon a
summer day, when the sun is about the hottest, I have remarked the same wind
arising and uttering the same, hollow, solemn, Memnonian, but saintly swell; it
is in this world the one sole *audible* symbol of eternity. And three times in my life
I have happened to hear the same sound in the same circumstances, namely,
when standing between an open window and a dead body on a summer day.[32]

That experience fixed forever the course of De Quincey's life as a
dark journey, alone, through a world of shadow and strange phantoms:

O Ahasuerus, everlasting Jew! Fable or not a fable, thou when first starting on
thy endless pilgrimage of woe . . . couldst not more certainly have read thy doom
of sorrow in the misgivings of thy troubled brain than I when passing forever
from my sister's room. The worm was at my heart, and confining myself to that
state of life, I may say, the worm that could not die.[33]

From that moment forth De Quincey felt himself alone on his continuing quest, his endless pilgrimage of woe. Although he had eight
children, and loved his wife dearly, she too died in the pattern of
feminine loss that seemed to be his destiny. Grief and solitude were his
true companions, although on the surface he always maintained his
exquisite courtesy and struggled manfully to meet his obligations and
support his family:

O grief! Thou art classed amongst the depressing passions. And true it is that
thou humblest to the dust, but also thou exaltest to the clouds. . . . Interesting it
is to observe how certainly all deep feelings agree in this, that they seek for
solitude and are nursed by solitude. Deep grief, deep love, how naturally do

[32] De Quincey, *Confessions*, 129, 131.   [33] Ibid. 133.

these ally themselves with religious feeling; and all three—love, grief, religion
—are haunters of solitary places. Love, grief, the passion of reverie, or the
mystery of devotion—what were these without solitude? All day long, when it
was not impossible for me to do so, I sought the most silent and sequestered
nooks in the grounds about the house or in the neighboring fields. . . . I wearied
the heavens with my inquest of beseeching looks. I tormented the blue depths
with obstinate scrutiny, sweeping them with my eyes and searching them forever
after one angelic face . . .[34]

Solitude, under the authority of Rousseau, of Senancour, of
Wordsworth, was a chief criterion of the Romantic sensibility. None,
however, bore deeper witness to the awesome domain of solitude than
De Quincey, his knowledge earned by the overwhelming experience of
his loss:

O burden of solitude, that cleavest to man through every stage of his being! In
his birth, which *has* been, in his life, which *is*, in his death, which *shall*
be—mighty and essential solitude that wast, and art, and art to be, thou broodest
like the spirit of God moving upon the surface of the deeps, over every heart that
sleeps in the nurseries of Christendom. . . . Deep is the solitude in life of
millions upon millions, who, with hearts welling forth love, have none to love
them. Deep is the solitude of those who, with secret griefs, have none to pity
them. Deep is the solitude of those who, fighting with doubts or darkness, have
none to counsel them. But deeper than the deepest of these solitudes is that
which broods over childhood, bringing before it, at intervals, the final solitude
which watches for it and is waiting for it within the gates of death.[35]

The organ tones of De Quincey's prose style here obliterate completely the image of the diminutive man, and replace it with Baudelaire's
admonition of our duty of respect for 'so serious an author'. But De
Quincey's dark journey through existence had only a dark hope to
sustain its quest:

Forever I searched the abysses with some wandering thoughts unintelligible
to myself. Forever I dallied with some obscure notion, how my sister's loss might
be made in some dim way available for delivering me from misery, or else how
the misery I had suffered and was suffering might be made, in some way equally
dim, the ransom for winning back her love.[36]

One of those dim ways in which he attempted to regain his
relationship with his sister was the poignant relationship with the
London waif, Ann. As with the earlier relationship, this one followed the
De Quinceyan pattern, or destiny rather, of loss. Baudelaire, with his

[34] Ibid. 136, 137.   [35] Ibid. 140.   [36] Ibid. 162.

profound insight, conjectures that 'if we were to make a philosophical comparison of the works of an artist with the condition of his soul when he was a child, would it not be simple to prove that genius is nothing more than childhood, precisely formulated, and now endowed with powerfully virile instruments of self-expression?'[37] At any rate, De Quincey's work, and the most central events of his later life, seem intensively to recapitulate his earliest forming experience. The story here about 'one famishing scholar and a neglected child' seems dream-like and existential, certainly mythical and iconic in its shared loneliness in the dark city.[38]

Arriving in London at the age of 18, De Quincey fell in with the youthful prostitute, Ann, whose last name he never knew, as she walked the streets:

Being myself at that time, of necessity, a peripatetic, or a walker of the streets, I naturally fell in more frequently with those female peripatetics, who are technically called street-walkers. . . . For many weeks I had walked at nights with this poor friendless girl up and down Oxford Street or had rested with her on steps and under the shelter of porticoes. She could not be so old as myself; she told me, indeed, that she had not completed her sixteenth year.[39]

Baudelaire speaks of this event from De Quincey's journey in this way: 'the young man had another friend, and it is time for us to speak of her. If I were to pen this narrative in a manner truly worthy of it, I should have to pluck a feather from an angel's wing, so chaste and filled with candour, grace, and pity do I find this episode.'[40] Baudelaire further notes that 'Ann was not one of those dazzling, brazen beauties whose demon eyes gleam through the fog, and who make a virtue of their shamelessness. Ann was a completely plain and simple creature, neglected and thrown off like so many others, and reduced to total abjection by false play.'[41]

The famishing scholar and the homeless waif mutually supported one another in their dream-like progress through the dark city. De Quincey recalls,

One night when we were pacing slowly along Oxford Street, and after a day when I had felt unusually ill and faint, I requested her to turn off with me into Soho Square. . . . Suddenly, as we sat, I grew much worse. . . . Then it was, at this crisis of my fate, that my poor orphan companion, who had herself met with little but injuries in this world, stretched out a saving hand to me. Uttering a cry

---

[37] *Baudelaire*, i. 498.   [38] De Quincey, *Confessions*, 41.   [39] Ibid. 42.
[40] *Baudelaire*, i. 455–6.   [41] Ibid. 456.

of terror, but without a moment's delay, she ran into Oxford Street, and in less time than could be imagined, returned to me with a glass of port wine and spices that acted upon my empty stomach . . . with an instantaneous power of restoration. . . . O youthful benefactress! How often in succeeding years, standing in solitary places and thinking of thee with grief of heart and perfect love, how often have I wished that . . . the benediction of a heart oppressed with gratitude . . . might have power given to it from above to chase, to haunt, to waylay, to overtake, to pursue thee into the central darkness of a London brothel or . . . into the darkness of the grave, there to awaken thee with an authentic message of peace and forgiveness and of final reconciliation![42]

Having to leave London to raise funds for his continued survival, De Quincey proceeds into one of his characteristic stylistic digressions, from which he returns to take up the story of Ann, become now another icon of the loss of the feminine:

Meantime, what had become of poor Ann? . . . . I sought her daily and waited for her every night. . . . I inquired for her of everyone who was likely to know her. . . . She had few acquaintances; most people, besides, thought that the earnestness of my inquiries arose from motives which moved their laughter or their slight regard; and others, thinking that I was in chase of a girl who had robbed me of some trifles, were naturally and excusably indisposed to give me any clue to her . . .[43]

At the conclusion of the episode De Quincey launches into one of the keening and sighing passages, perfumed and evocative, that have forever been associated with the special kind of prose poetry in which he speaks of loss:

. . . to this hour, I have never heard a syllable about her. This, amongst such troubles as most men meet with in this life, has been my heaviest affliction. If she lived, doubtless we must have been sometimes in search of each other, at the very same moment, through the mighty labyrinths of London, perhaps even within a few feet of each other—a barrier no wider, in a London street, often amounting in the end to a separation for eternity! . . . So, then Oxford Street, stony-hearted stepmother . . . at length I was dismissed from thee! . . . Successors, too many, to myself and Ann have, doubtless, since then trodden in our footsteps, inheritors of our calamities; other orphans than Ann have sighed, tears have been shed by other children; and thou, Oxford Street, has since echoed to the groans of innumerable hearts.[44]

But then, seventeen years later, De Quincey symbolically retrieves Ann even from the darkness of the grave; he rejoins her in a dream of resurrection. It was, he thought, an Easter Sunday, 'the day on which they celebrate the first fruits of resurrection. . . . And not a bow-shot

---

[42] De Quincey, *Confessions*, 43–4.   [43] Ibid. 55.   [44] Ibid. 56.

from me, upon a stone, and shaded by Judaean palms, there sat a
woman; and I looked, and it was—Ann!'[45] And to the figure he speaks
only the few affecting words: 'So, then, I have found you at last.'[46] The
entirety of his life's quest and heart's wanting is recapitulated in that
scene and in those words, to be recapitulated ever again as he ever-again
writes his truth.

Ann was not the only waif who focused the ideal of feminine
childhood during De Quincey's journey through the dark labyrinths of
London. He recounts another episode, existentially and symbolically
similar to that of Ann:

. . . when cold and more inclement weather came on, and when, from the length
of my sufferings, I had begun to sink into a more languishing condition, it was,
no doubt, fortunate for me that the same person to whose breakfast table I had
access allowed me to sleep in a large, unoccupied house of which he was
tenant. . . . But I found, on taking possession of my new quarters, that the house
already contained one single inmate, a poor friendless child, apparently ten years
old. . . . From this forlorn child I learned that she had slept and lived there alone
for some time before I came; and great joy the poor creature expressed when she
found that I was in future to be her companion. . . . We lay upon the floor with a
bundle of crushed law papers for a pillow, but with no other covering than a sort
of large horseman's cloak; afterwards, however, we discovered in a garret, an old
sofa cover, a small piece of rug, and some fragments of other articles, which
added a little to our warmth. The poor child crept close to me for warmth and for
security against her ghostly enemies. When I was not more than usually ill, I took
her into my arms so that, in general, she was tolerably warm and often slept when
I could not . . .[47]

This child, like Ann, was one of Levana's delegations. An especially
interesting delegation of that kind was De Quincey's intense love for
Wordsworth's daughter, Catharine, she of the beautiful sonnet,
'Surprised by Joy', and it is a remarkable and touching fact that this little
girl, whose death aroused such profound grief in her father, aroused if
possible even more in De Quincey.[48]

[45] Ibid. 98.   [46] Ibid.   [47] Ibid. 38–9.
[48] As De Quincey says of Catharine's death: 'Never, perhaps, from the foundations of
those mighty hills, was there so fierce a convulsion of grief as mastered my faculties on
receiving that heart-shattering news' (*De Quincey*, ii. 443). For additional statements see
pp. 441–5. Cf. Robinson: 'At chambers I was unexpectedly visited by Wordsworth. He
was come up from Bocking suddenly in consequence of tidings of the sudden death of his
daughter, Catherine, a girl of four years of age, and he was going to Wales to Mrs
Wordsworth. His spirits were properly affected, and his language that which became a
man both of feeling and strength of mind. I walked with him to Coleridge, and he called on
a Mr De Quincey, a friend who had lately visited the Lakes, and was greatly attached to the
little girl. Mr De Quincey burst into tears on seeing Wordsworth and seemed to be more
affected than the father' (*Robinson*, i. 103. 11 June 1812).

We surely know why. The death of Catharine Wordsworth was a recapitulation of the death of Elizabeth De Quincey. The loss of Ann was a recapitulation of that death as well. As De Quincey says of his parting from Ann:

I loved her as affectionately as if she had been my sister, and at this moment with sevenfold tenderness from pity at witnessing her extreme dejection. . . . [W]hen I kissed her at our final farewell, she put her arms about my neck and wept, without speaking a word. I hoped to return in a week at furthest, and I agreed with her that on the fifth night from that, and every night afterwards, she should wait for me at six o'clock near the bottom of Great Titchfield Street, which had been our customary haven, as it were, of rendezvous, to prevent our missing each other in the great Mediterranean of Oxford Street.[49]

But he did miss her, and his quest continued. It could only cease with his death. He did many things in his life of mental wandering (interestingly, he never physically travelled outside the British Isles), but underneath his cheerful spirits were the grief and the search:

And howsoever a man may think that he is without hope, I, that have read the writing upon these great abysses of grief and viewed their shadows under the correction of mightier shadows from deeper abysses since then, abysses of aboriginal fear and eldest darkness, in which yet I believe that all hope had not absolutely died, know that he is in a natural error. . . . [D]espair . . . the anguish of darkness, was not *essential* to such sorrow, but might come and go even as light comes and goes upon our troubled earth.[50]

When his sister died, and while he was talking of the endless pilgrimage of woe, he had said:

Some passions, as that of sexual love, are celestial by one half of their origin, animal and earthly by the other half. . . . But love, which is *altogether* holy, like that between two children, will revisit undoubtedly by glimpses the silence and the darkness of old age, and I repeat my belief—that unless bodily torment should forbid it, that final experience in my sister's bedroom . . . will rise again for me, to illuminate the hour of death.[51]

It did rise again, to illuminate the hour of death. As reported in some memories of De Quincey's final hours, written by one of his daughters for his nineteenth-century biographer, Alexander Japp, De Quincey finally came home to the eternal feminine and especially to his sister:

He had for hours ceased to recognize any of us, but we heard him murmur, though quite distinctly, 'My dear, dear mother. Then I was greatly mistaken.' Then as the waves of death rolled faster and faster over him, suddenly out of the

[49] De Quincey, *Confessions*, 49.   [50] Ibid. 145.   [51] Ibid. 133.

abyss we saw him throw up his arms, which to the last retained their strength, and say distinctly, and as if in great surprise, 'Sister! sister! sister!'[52]

De Quincey always felt that the wound he suffered from the death of his sister Jane, though, as he put it, 'the first wound in my infant heart',[53] had healed. But the wound of Elizabeth's loss never healed, and his frame shook forever after from the shock of 'God's thunderbolt at my heart in the assurance that my sister *must* die'.[54]

The special prose style that he developed to cauterize and bind up the wound is a never-ending wonder, and no one has described it with more conscious attempts to isolate its sinuous and meandering movement, its movement of binding-up, as it were, than did De Quincey himself. He says in the Introductory Notice to *Suspiria de Profundis* (and though the medical imagery purports to relate to opium, its subtext is the deeper relation to the sickness of his sister):

I tell my critic that the whole course of this narrative resembles, and was meant to resemble, a *caduceus* wreathed about with meandering ornaments or the shaft of a tree's stem hung round and surmounted with some vagrant parasitical plant. The mere medical subject of the opium answers to the dry, withered pole, which shoots all the rings of the flowering plants and seems to do so by some dexterity of its own, whereas, in fact, the plant and its tendrils have curled round the sullen cylinder by mere luxuriance of *theirs*. The true object in my *Opium Confessions* is not the naked physiological theme—on the contrary, that is the ugly pole . . .—but those wandering musical variations upon the theme, those parasitical thoughts, feelings, digressions, which climb up with bells and blossoms around the arid stock . . .[55]

From antiquity on, the caduceus has been the symbol of the healer, and the style it symbolizes here, we can scarcely doubt, was meant to be a healing also.

Remarkably, however, this haunting style is not De Quincey's only, nor even his only *virtuoso*, style. Hazlitt, too, is a stylist, a supreme stylist even, but Hazlitt has only one style; whereas it is difficult to think of another figure with so varied a stylistic repertoire as De Quincey. The style he uses in his startling piece on 'Murder Considered as One of the Fine Arts' is taut, reportorial, and suspenseful, a world removed from

[52] H. A. Page, *Thomas De Quincey: His Life and Writings. With Unpublished Correspondence* (New York: Scribner, Armstrong & Co., 1877), ii. 305. Another version is less dramatic: 'Once he called out loud and distinctly, "Florence, Florence, Florence." [One of De Quincey's daughters.] Once we heard him say, "Sister, Sister". I heard him once say, "My dear dear Mother." To the last he called us, "My love" . . . I never heard such a pathos as there was in it . . .' (Letter of Emily De Quincey to James T. Fields, 12 Dec. 1859, in *De Quincey at Work*, 43).   [53] De Quincey, *Confessions*, 125.
[54] Ibid. 128.   [55] Ibid. 120.

the caduceus style. The style he uses in his *Recollections of the Lakes and the Lake Poets* is conversational, anecdotal, frequently humorous.

His recollections of the lake poets, and under this rubric I include all the articles produced upon that theme, are especially important productions not only in themselves, but also in that they reveal another side of De Quincey's experience, his masculine relationships. The dream quest, orientated towards the feminine, had to glide along rails laid down in the quotidian obligations of men. Even a journey to the end of night requires a road bedded in mundane reality. Such a track is marked out in the concerns of his recollections. For the memories of Wordsworth and Coleridge, of Southey too, that were harvested to form their substance arose from De Quincey's participation in the world of masculine peers and rivals, and they were memories of the most important non-feminine relationships of De Quincey's life.

His recollections bring into focus an enormous and long-standing commitment on De Quincey's part both to Wordsworth and to Coleridge. To be sure, the tendency to reveal intimate and personal details, which in our own day seems quite proper, loosed a fire-storm of rebuke on their author's head, particularly with regard to the portrait of Coleridge that appeared shortly after Coleridge's death. 'I have been reading three articles on Coleridge in *Tait's Magazine*,' writes Crabb Robinson in December 1834, 'in which De Quincey, with the show of intense admiration both of Wordsworth and Coleridge, nevertheless relates anecdotes and indulges in comments incompatible with respect, to say nothing of gratitude. It is deplorable that men of talent like De Quincey, under the pressure of want, should seize on the reputation of a deceased friend as a prey, turning his personal acquaintance with them to profit.'[56] Later Sara Coleridge, in more tactful disapproval, noted that De Quincey 'does not write well on personal points, though admirably always, when he keeps away from the *Maremma* or Snake Marsh of private anecdote.'[57] 'Had Coleridge been alive,' remarked Julius Hare more acidly, De Quincey 'would not have dared thus to prate and chatter about him.'[58] Wordsworth was alive, and Wordsworth was furious.[59] He

[56] *Robinson*, i. 451.
[57] Sara Coleridge, 'Introduction' to *Biographia Literaria* 2nd edn. (London: William Pickering, 1847), i. cxxxv.
[58] J. C. H[are], 'Samuel Taylor Coleridge and the English Opium-Eater', *The British Magazine and Monthly Register of Religion and Ecclesiastical Information*, 7 (1835), 21.
[59] But even so, perhaps not so furious as Southey: "'I have told Hartley Coleridge", said he, "tha' he ought to take a strong cudgel, proceed straight to Edinburgh, and give De Quincey, publicly in the streets there, a sound beating, as a calumniator, cowardly spy, traitor, base betrayer of the hospitable social hearth . . . !"' (Carlyle, *Reminiscences*, 324).

had always been reticent about his personal life, successfully urging Barron Field not to publish his wholly admiring memoirs of the poet. Wordsworth read Field's manuscript in 1840 and wrote to Moxon: 'I set my face entirely against the publication of Mr Field's MSS';[60] and to Field himself he wrote that he was 'decidedly against the publication of your Critical Memoir' and that 'it is far better not to admit people so much behind the scenes, as it has been lately fashionable to do.'[61]

Wordsworth was certainly referring here, at least in part, to De Quincey. To Alexander Dyce he wrote: 'De Quincey the opium-eater is a person of great intellect and great attainments; I am sorry to add that he is a great liar and rascal: he has lately contributed to *Tait's Magazine* a series of papers on Coleridge, which are full of the grossest falsehoods.'[62]

One could scarcely gather from this acerbic opinion how idolatrously De Quincey had regarded Wordsworth, worked for him, slaved for him even. In 1803, when in his eighteenth year, De Quincey had said that the 'far holier idols of my heart' were 'the joint poems of Wordsworth and Coleridge',[63] and when he was 'under twenty years of age' his 'admiration for Coleridge (as, in perhaps a still greater degree, for Wordsworth) was literally in no respect short of a religious feeling'.[64]

Needing a father, De Quincey adopted Wordsworth. He introduced himself to the great poet by a tactful letter,[65] and in due course he moved to the Lake District to be near Wordsworth, stressing his son-ship by moving into Dove Cottage as tenant when the Wordsworths moved out.[66] Indeed, his unbounded affection for Wordsworth's daughter, Catharine, no doubt was fuelled by the unconscious belief that as Wordsworth's surrogate son he could claim her as an actual sister.

But the perils of the father–son relationship can be illustrated by the fact that De Quincey, with monumental clumsiness (he was here certainly far closer to Don Quixote in his clumsiest misapprehensions of reality than to Parzival or Galahad), offended the Wordsworths to the heart by a singular demonstration of hostility to nature, a demonstration so singular, indeed, that one has to find profound unconscious aggression in it. The Wordsworths had been glad of their young friend's

---

[60] *Barron Field's Memoirs of Wordsworth*, ed. Geoffrey Little (Sydney: Sydney University Press for the Australian Academy of the Humanities, 1975), 16.   [61] Ibid. 17.
[62] Samuel Schoenbaum, 'Dyce's Recollections of Wordsworth, Mrs. Siddons, and Other Notable Persons', *TLS* (2 Jan. 1971), 102.   [63] *De Quincey*, iii. 36.
[64] Ibid. 41.   [65] For the letter, dated 31 May 1803, see Jordan, 30–1.
[66] As Dorothy Wordsworth said of De Quincey, 'he is like one of our own Family' (*Middle Years*, i. 376).

occupancy of Dove Cottage and the implied son-ship that went with it: 'we have now almost a home still', said Dorothy, 'at the old and dearest spot of all.'[67] With incredible insensitivity, however, De Quincey began to vandalize the garden. Sara Hutchinson reports the matter in scandalized tones: 'What do you say to de Q[uincey]'s having polled the Ash Tree & cut down the hedge all round the orchard—every Holly, Heckberry, Hazel, and every twig that skreened it—& all for the sake of the Apple trees that he may have a few more Apples.'[68] One cannot do that sort of thing to a nature-loving Wordsworth. Dorothy, reported Sara, 'is so hurt and angry that she can never speak to him more: & truly it was a most unfeeling thing when he knew how much store they set by that orchard—the Apple trees also are so pruned that instead of its being a little wood, as it used to be, there is neither shade or shelter'.[69] So Wordsworth discovered, long before the formulations of Freud, that fatherhood has its dangers.

Yet Wordsworth certainly gave as good as he got. Those who wish to pursue in detail the fascinating, instructive, and ultimately melancholy story of the two men's relationship should consult John E. Jordan's *De Quincey to Wordsworth: A Biography of a Relationship, with the Letters of Thomas De Quincey to the Wordsworth Family*. Here we shall confine ourselves to one example, De Quincey's report of Wordsworth's characteristic ability to be insulting to those outside his circle:

Upon ground where he was really strong, Wordsworth was not arrogant. In a question of criticism, he was open to any man's suggestions. But there *were* fields of thought or of observation which he seemed to think locked up and sacred to himself; and any alien entrance upon those fields he treated almost as intrusions and usurpations. . . . Wordsworth virtually claimed the same precedency for all who were connected with himself. . . . To everybody standing out of this sacred and privileged pale Wordsworth behaved with absolute insult in cases of this

[67] Ibid. 19 Nov. 1809.
[68] *The Letters of Sara Hutchinson*, ed. Kathleen Coburn (Toronto: University of Toronto Press, 1954), 36. 3 Dec. 1811.
[69] Ibid. 36–7. The blow was especially severe to Dorothy, because she had happily written to De Quincey some two years before and said, 'Pleasant indeed it is to think of that little orchard which for one seven years at least will be a secure covert for the Birds, and undisturbed by the woodman's ax. There is no other spot which we may have prized year after year that we can ever look upon without apprehension that next year, next month, or even to-morrow it may be deformed and ravaged' (*Middle Years*, i. 337–8. 6 May 1809). Dorothy's express fears (later in the letter she speaks of great trees cut down by avarice: 'but *malice* has done the work, and the trees are levelled' (338)) make De Quincey's action even more unmistakably symbolic of aggression, especially in view of the fact that in his letter of introduction to William in 1803 he had said that his 'life has been passed chiefly in the contemplation and altogether in the worship of nature' (Jordan, 31).

nature: he did not even appear to listen; but as if what they said on such a theme must be childish prattle, turned away with an air of perfect indifference; began talking, perhaps, with another person on another subject; or, at all events never noticed what we said by an apology for an answer. I, very early in our connexion, having observed this inhuman arrogance, took care never afterwards to lay myself under the possibility of such an insult.[70]

As De Quincey later wryly says, 'Never describe Wordsworth as equal in pride to Lucifer: no, but, if you have occasion to write a life of Lucifer, set down that by possibility, in respect to pride, he might be some type of Wordsworth.'[71]

De Quincey's relationship to Coleridge was different. Wordsworth was a father, Coleridge was a brother. 'He was, in a literary sense, our brother', wrote De Quincey.[72] A brother in a psychological sense also, somewhat unfortunately for Coleridge. De Quincey's Oedipal aggression struck deep at Wordsworth's garden; his sibling rivalry and fraternally Oedipal aggression skewered Coleridge as well, for it was De Quincey who broached the plagiarism charges against Coleridge. In his articles of 1834, shortly after Coleridge's death, De Quincey said that Thomas Poole (Poole perplexedly denied it)[73] 'furnished me with the first hint of a singular infirmity besetting Coleridge's mind',[74] and De Quincey proceeds to set forth a conversation between himself and Poole in which Poole mentions that 'our dear excellent friend Coleridge, than whom God never made a creature more divinely endowed . . . sometimes steals from other people, just as you or I might do'.[75]

De Quincey's older brother, William, had been of a notably aggressive temperament, and the younger and slighter De Quincey might be forgiven for having learned at least a covert aggression in return. And Coleridge was not only a brother figure, but even an *alter ego*, a kind of 'Dark Interpreter', to use De Quincey's own pregnant conception, from

---

[70] De Quincey, *Recollections*, 375–6. Perhaps an additional illustration will be useful. Wordsworth was contemptuous of Charles Lloyd, while De Quincey was sympathetic to him. 'I put a question [about Lloyd's illness] . . . when to my surprise (my wrath internally, but also to my special amusement), [Wordsworth] replied that, in fact, what he had said was a matter of some delicacy, and not quite proper to be communicated except to *near friends of the family*. This to me!—O ye gods!—to me, who knew by many a hundred conversations how disagreeable Wordsworth was both to Charles Lloyd and his wife. . . . The arrogance of Wordsworth was well illustrated in this case of the Lloyds' (ibid. 320).
[71] Ibid. 381.   [72] *De Quincey*, v. 181.
[73] 'As for the conversation he states as having had with me, I am sure *it must be incorrect*, for as I never considered Coleridge as a Plagiarist, I never could have said what he has given me' (Mrs Henry Sandford, *Thomas Poole and His Friends* (London: Macmillan and Co., 1888), ii. 305).   [74] De Quincey, *Recollections*, 36.   [75] Ibid.

whom the younger man had to separate himself to gain identity.[76] Hazlitt had had to reject Coleridge also in order to find intellectual adulthood, but De Quincey's similarity to Coleridge was much closer than Hazlitt's, his admiration for Coleridge no less, and his need for self-definition accordingly even greater, though that self-definition proceeded differently, in terms of De Quincey's idiosyncratic strategies for dealing with the world.

De Quincey and Coleridge were alike in remarkable ways. Both suffered in infancy from rather cold and distant mothers; both were dominated by older brothers; both left university without a degree— Coleridge from Jesus College, Cambridge, De Quincey from Worcester College, Oxford; both were inveterate readers; both immersed themselves in German culture; both were 'at once systematic and labyrinthine' in their intellectual procedures (the phrase is one that Coleridge himself used to describe De Quincey's mind);[77] both were procrastinators; both were plagiarists (Albert Goldman documents the irony, as it were, in De Quincey's statement that Coleridge 'steals from other people, just as you or I might do').[78] Both, finally, were opium addicts.

Even here, indeed, De Quincey had to free himself from Coleridge. The *Opium Confessions* by which his fame was made conferred on De Quincey the identity of the 'Opium-Eater', changed him from a nonentity into a famous man. But Coleridge could have claimed the same identity. To forestall this possibility in the public mind, De Quincey said in the *Confessions of an English Opium-Eater* that 'This is the doctrine of the true church on the subject of opium: of which church I acknowledge myself to be the only member,—the alpha and omega.'[79] But he knew better. As he records of his very first conversations with Coleridge:

At night he entered into a spontaneous explanation of this unhappy overclouding of his life, on occasion of my saying accidentally that a toothache had obliged

---

[76] The 'Dark Interpreter', like the Brocken Spectre, was 'originally a mere reflex of my inner nature. But as the apparition of the Brocken sometimes is disturbed by storms or driving showers, so as to dissemble his real origin, in like manner the Interpreter sometimes swerves out of my orbit and mixes a little with alien natures. I do not know him in these cases as my own parhelion' (De Quincey, *Confessions*, 182). For the proximity of the 'Dark Interpreter' to De Quincey's awareness of Coleridge, see Robert M. Maniquis, 'The Dark Interpreter and the Palimpsest of Violence: De Quincey and the Unconscious', *Thomas De Quincey: Bicentenary Studies*, ed. Robert Lance Snyder (Norman and London: University of Oklahoma Press, 1985), 109–39.

[77] Coleridge, *Letters*, iii. 205. 2 May 1809.

[78] Albert Goldman, *The Mine and the Mint: Sources for the Writings of Thomas De Quincey* (Carbondale, Ill.: Southern Illinois University Press, 1965).

[79] De Quincey, *Confessions*, 64.

me to take a few drops of laudanum. At what time or on what motive he had commenced the use of opium, he did not say; but the peculiar emphasis of horror with which he warned me against forming a habit of the same kind impressed upon my mind a feeling that he never hoped to liberate himself from the bondage.[80]

Indeed, the freedom with which De Quincey wrote about Coleridge's opium addiction, after his own identity as the Opium-Eater had been incontrovertibly established, was one of the things about his recollections that most scandalized Coleridge's friends.[81]

It must not be supposed, however, from these evidences of De Quincey's rivalry with Coleridge, that he did not respect his older friend. Both Hazlitt and Lamb were dazzled by Coleridge; neither of them, however, their awed reactions notwithstanding, held his powers in higher veneration than did De Quincey. Even before he met Coleridge, De Quincey, after hearing some anecdotes by two people who knew the poet, walked home 'thinking of *Coleridge*;—am in transports of love and admiration for him. . . . I begin to think him the greatest man that has ever appeared.'[82] He still thought so in 1834, when his recollections of Coleridge were published, because they begin with a tribute that can never be surpassed for anyone. For Coleridge is there called 'this illustrious man, the largest and most spacious intellect, the subtlest and most comprehensive, in my judgment, that has yet existed among men.'[83] At the end of the series, De Quincey judges that though Goethe was 'more widely celebrated' than Coleridge, this greatest of German writers was 'far his inferior in power and compass of intellect.'[84]

Even after detailing the plagiarism charges, De Quincey both demonstrates his sense of rivalry with Coleridge and simultaneously asserts Coleridge's unbounded merit:

I will assert finally that, after having read for thirty years in the same track as Coleridge—that track in which few of any age will ever follow us, such as German metaphysicians, Latin schoolmen, thaumaturgic Platonists, religious Mystics,—and having thus discovered a large variety of trivial thefts, I do,

---

[80] De Quincey, *Recollections*, 56. For perhaps the most revealing of all surveys of the havoc wrought by opium not only upon Coleridge's work, but upon his personal relationships and, most poignantly, upon those who necessarily relied upon him, see Molly LeFebure, *The Bondage of Love: A Life of Mrs Samuel Taylor Coleridge* (London: Victor Gollancz Ltd., 1986).

[81] De Quincey did not confine himself to the initial articles of 1834 occasioned by Coleridge's death. See, for example, the article of 1845 called 'Coleridge and Opium-Eating', *De Quincey*, v. 179–214.   [82] De Quincey, *Diary*, 191–2.

[83] De Quincey, *Recollections*, 33.   [84] Ibid. 111.

nevertheless, most heartily believe him to have been as entirely original in all his capital pretensions as any one man that ever has existed.[85]

Where almost all Coleridge's English peers—Byron, Wordsworth, even Hazlitt—deprecated Coleridge's involvement in German metaphysics, De Quincey hailed that involvement and made it a further area of fellow-feeling: 'it had crowned the interest which to me invested his name,' he writes about the time before he even knew Coleridge, '—that about the year 1804 or 1805 I had been informed by a gentleman from the English Lakes, who knew him as a neighbour, that he had for some time applied his whole mind to metaphysics and psychology,—which happened to be my own absorbing pursuit.'[86] Elsewhere De Quincey sees Coleridge as being enlarged rather than diminished by his metaphysical preoccupation:

This astonishing man, be it again remembered, besides being an exquisite poet, a profound political speculator, a philosophic student of literature through all its chambers and recesses, was also a circumnavigator on the most pathless waters of scholasticism and metaphysics. He had sounded, without guiding charts, the secret depths of Proclus and Plotinus; he had laid down buoys on the twilight or moonlight ocean of Jacob Boehmen; he had cruised over the broad Atlantic of Kant and Schelling, of Fichte and Oken. Where is the man who shall be equal to these things?[87]

It seems clear that De Quincey rather thought that he himself was the man equal to those things. A curious aspect of his writings is the self-congratulatory stance he repeatedly assumes: he is continually telling us how early he learned Greek and how good his Greek is, how adept he is at Latin, how much he knows about German literature and thought, how much he reads, and how well he thinks. Equally curious is the fact that this self-promotion rarely irritates one as egotism, but seems on the contrary the almost lovable foible of a gentle and extraordinarily intelligent man. Perhaps it is because De Quincey speaks so well and accurately of others that his self-promotion does not grate on us. His justness of observation and judgement makes him the best and most penetrating of all those who have essayed biographical presentation of Coleridge, as well as one of the best on Wordsworth.

In any event, his praise and admiration of Coleridge continually imply their recapitulations in De Quincey's own intellectual life. Coleridge, for instance, knew Kant more thoroughly than any man in England.

[85] Ibid. 40–1.   [86] Ibid. 34.   [87] De Quincey, v. 182–3.

Eventually De Quincey came to occupy a nearly similar position. Many passing remarks, as well as his piece called 'The Last Days of Immanuel Kant', his piece on 'Kant in his Miscellaneous Essays', the one on 'Kant's idea of a Universal History on a Cosmopolitan Plan', and his essay 'On the English Notices of Kant' (this last a prefiguration of Wellek's *Kant in England* much later), demonstrate involvement in the whole of Kant's life and work.[88]

This tendency to recapitulative structures, noted earlier in the various delegations of sister relationships under the symbolism of Levana, is most strikingly apparent in the last of De Quincey's productions to be considered in this chapter, his essay on 'The English Mail Coach'. No other statement, indeed not even the great passages of the *Suspiria de Profundis*, seems so surely to recapitulate his life as a journey to the end of night. Nor is any other work so remarkable in its tone, progression, and import as this one. Coleridge once spoke of Berkeley's *Siris* as beginning with Tar-water and ending with the Trinity. The same kind of thing may be said of 'The English Mail Coach'. It begins with commonplace and ends with apocalypse.

It surely does not seem at the outset as though the essay will provide a journey to the end of night. It begins with the kind of comfortable sense of commonplace occasion raised to popularity by Addison; though if we have prior awareness of De Quincey's own journey to the end of night, the title of the first section, 'The Glory of Motion', might have a certain proleptic vibration to it. But the opening is purely that of the conversational essay, with some of the humdrum detail of which Swift was the master:

Some twenty or more years before I matriculated at Oxford, Mr Palmer, at that time MP for Bath, had accomplished two things very hard to do on our little planet . . . he had invented mail coaches, and he had married the daughter of a duke. He was, therefore, just twice as great a man as Galileo, who did certainly invent (or, which is the same thing, discover) the satellites of Jupiter, those very next things extant to mail coaches in the two capital pretensions of speed and

---

[88] See in addition 'Kant on National Character in Relation to the Sense of the Sublime and Beautiful', 'Kant's Abstract of Swedenborgianism', and 'Kant on the Age of the Earth' (*De Quincey*, xiv); 'German Studies and Kant in Particular' (*De Quincey*, ii); 'The German Language, and Philosophy of Kant' (*The Uncollected Writings of Thomas De Quincey*, ed. James Hogg (London: Swan Sonnenschein; New York: Macmillan, 1892), i. 91–129). Carlyle, whom Goethe once praised as almost more at home in German literature than the Germans themselves ('wie hat er uns Deutsche studiert! Er ist in unserer Literatur fast besser zu Hause als wir selbst' (*Goethe*, xxiv. 293)), wrote: 'You'll find De Quincey a man of very considerable genius. . . . He also is a German, a Kantist' (Carlyle, *Letters*, iv. 30).

keeping time, but, on the other hand, who did *not* marry the daughter of a duke.[89]

The wry, chuckling style, so unlike the tone of Levana and the Ladies of Sorrow, seems to imply the vignettes of Hazlitt or the whimsy of Lamb. In line with this expectation we are soon at Oxford under the care of a rueful young De Quincey:

The mail coach . . . became itself a spiritualized and glorified object to an impassioned heart; and naturally, in the Oxford of that day, *all* hearts were impassioned, as being all (or nearly all) in *early* manhood. In most universities there is one single college; in Oxford there were five and twenty, all of which were peopled by young men, the *élite* of their own generation[90] . . .

The number, twenty-five, heralds a preoccupation with counting, slowing the pace to Swiftian specificity:

In some of these many colleges the custom permitted the student to keep what are called 'short terms', that is, the four terms of Michaelmas, Lent, Easter, and Act were kept by a residence, in the aggregate, of ninety-one days, or thirteen weeks. Under this interrupted residence it was possible that a student might have a reason for going down to his home four times in the year. This made eight journeys to and fro. But, as these homes lay dispersed through all the shires of the island, and most of us disdained all coaches except his majesty's mail, no city out of London could pretend to so extensive a connexion with Mr Palmer's establishment as Oxford. Three mails, at the least, I remember as passing every day through Oxford and benefiting by my personal patronage—viz., the Worcester, the Gloucester, and the Holyhead mail.[91]

Sedately pawing the ground, as it were, this passage prepares our expectation for an ambling series of humorous evocations much like the comfortable pace of the coach as it jogs along from station to station. De Quincey brilliantly focuses the expectation by his first vignette, which combines Lambian whimsy with Dickensian social presentation:

Up to this time, say 1804 or 1805 . . . it had been the fixed assumption of the four inside people . . . that they, the illustrious quaternion, constituted a porcelain variety of the human race, whose dignity would have been compromised by exchanging one word of civility with the three miserable delft-ware outsides. . . . What words, then, could express the horror and the sense of treason . . . where all three outsides (the trinity of Pariahs) made a vain attempt to sit down at the same breakfast-table or dinner-table with the consecrated four? . . . The course taken with the infatuated outsiders, in the particular attempt which I have noticed, was that the waiter, beckoning them away from the privileged *salle à*

---

[89] *De Quincey*, xiii. 270–1.   [90] Ibid. 272–3.   [91] Ibid. 273.

manger, sang out, 'This way, my good men', and then enticed these good men away to the kitchen. But that plan had not always answered. Sometimes, though rarely, cases occurred where the intruders . . . resolutely refused to budge, and so far carried their point as to have a separate table arranged for themselves in a corner of the general room. Yet, if an Indian screen could be found ample enough to plant them out from the very eyes of the high table, or *dais*, it then became possible to assume as a fiction of law that the three deft fellows, after all, were not present. They could be ignored by the porcelain men, under the maxim that objects not appearing and objects not existing are governed by the same logical construction.[92]

The vignette is quite perfect in its kind, exchanging an implied social criticism for whimsical amiability, and reinforcing a sense of comfort about the status quo of life not unlike that of the inn itself. It also serves as a transition to De Quincey's own self-definition as an outsider on the journey to be resumed:

Such being, at that time the usage of mail coaches, what was to be done by us of young Oxford? We, the most aristocratic of people, who were addicted to the practice of looking down superciliously even upon the insides themselves as often very questionable characters—were we, by voluntarily going outside, to court indignities? If our dress and bearing sheltered us generally from the suspicion of being 'raff' (the name at that period for 'snobs'), we really *were* such constructively by the place we assumed . . . [B]ut the outside of the mail had its own incommunicable advantages. These we could not forgo. . . . The air, the freedom of prospect, the proximity to the horses, the elevation of seat: these were what we required, but above all, the certain anticipation of purchasing occasional opportunities of driving. . . . [T]he *inside*, which had been traditionally regarded as the only room tenantable by gentlemen, was, in fact, the coal cellar in disguise.[93]

De Quincey then makes a leisurely and comfortable digression in an anecdote about China, still in the mode of Lamb, ending with the assurance that 'the state coach was dedicated thenceforward as a votive offering to the God Fo Fo—whom the learned more accurately called Fi Fi'.[94]

Continuing to maintain the co-ordinates of comfort and whimsy, the essay, like the coach, jogs on, only occasionally glimpsing, from its ordered society, the prospect of darker things:

It is felony to stop the mail; even the sheriff cannot do that. . . . No dignity is perfect which does not at some point ally itself with the mysterious. The connexion of the mail with the state and the executive government . . . gave to the whole mail establishment an official grandeur which did us service on the roads and invested us with seasonable terrors. . . . Look at those turnpike gates! With what deferential hurry . . . they fly open at our approach! Look at that long line of carts and carters ahead. . . . Ah! Traitors, they do not hear us as yet; but, as soon as the dreadful blast of our horn reaches them with proclamation of our approach, see with what frenzy of trepidation they fly to their horses' heads . . .[95]

The coach, with the 'dreadful blast' of its horn faintly foreshadowing the impending trumpet of apocalypse, gradually reveals itself, the mask of whimsy still in place but jiggling, as something of careering velocity: 'Sometimes after breakfast his Majesty's mail would . . . upset an apple cart, a cart loaded with eggs, etc. Huge was the affliction and dismay, awful was the smash.'[96] The sense of power and velocity is further enhanced by a Lambian vignette of passing another coach:

I remember being on the box of the Holyhead mail, between Shrewsbury and Oswestry, when a tawdry thing from Birmingham, some 'Tallyho' or 'High-flyer', all flaunting with green and gold, came up alongside of us. . . . For some time this Birmingham machine ran along by our side—a piece of familiarity that already of itself seemed to me sufficiently jacobinical. But all at once a movement of the horses announced a desperate intention of leaving us behind. 'Do you see *that?*' I said to the coachman.—'I see', was his short answer. He was wide awake,—yet he waited longer than seemed prudent; for the horses of our audacious opponent had a disagreeable air of freshness and power. But his motive was loyal; his wish was that the Birmingham conceit should be full-blown before he froze it. When *that* seemed right, he unloosed, or to speak by a stronger word, he *sprang*, his known resources: he slipped our royal horses like cheetahs, or hunting-leopards. . . . Passing them without an effort, as it seemed, we threw them into the rear with so lengthening an interval between us as proved in itself the bitterest mockery of their presumption, whilst our guard blew back a shattering blast of triumph that was really too painfully full of derision.[97]

Musing on velocity and power, De Quincey begins to delve beneath the surface:

The modern modes of travelling cannot compare with the old mail-coach system in grandeur and power. They boast of more velocity,—not, however, as a consciousness, but as a fact of our lifeless knowledge, resting upon *alien* evidence: as, for instance, because somebody *says* that we have gone fifty miles in the hour, though we are far from feeling it as a personal experience; or upon the evidence of a result, as that actually we find ourselves in York four hours after leaving London. . . . But, seated on the old mail-coach, we needed no evidence out of ourselves to indicate the velocity. . . . [W]e heard our speed, we saw it, we felt it as a thrilling; and this speed was not the product of blind insensate

---

[95] Ibid. 278, 279–80.   [96] Ibid. 280–1.   [97] Ibid. 281–2.

agencies . . . but was incarnated in the fiery eyeball of the noblest among brutes, in his dilated nostril, spasmodic muscles, and thunder-beating hoofs. . . . But now, on the new system of travelling, iron tubes and boilers have disconnected man's heart from the ministers of his locomotion.[98]

It is, indeed, the reconnection of the heart with the ministers of locomotion that emerges as the dominant motif of 'The English Mail Coach', and the representation of velocity throughout the piece is masterful and profound. The railway must be discredited as bearer of velocity, for the horses of De Quincey are to become the horses of the Apocalypse; no velocity has ever surpassed that of his mail-coach as it careers toward its appointment with the ultimate. That the essay is preparing to move into deeper and darker dimensions is suggested by a timely appearance of the eternal feminine, an iconic sister figure called 'sweet Fanny of the Bath road', who became 'the glorified inmate of my dreams', and a symbol of De Quinceyan loss: 'Fanny, as the loveliest young woman for face and person that perhaps in my whole life I have beheld':[99]

Miss Fanny of the Bath road, strictly speaking lived at a mile's distance from that road, but came so continually to meet the mail that I on my frequent transits rarely missed her. . . . The mail-coachman, who drove the Bath mail and wore the royal livery happened to be Fanny's grandfather.[100]

To emphasize the connection of this avatar of the eternal feminine with the careering progress of the coach, De Quincey dwells on the relation of grandfather to granddaughter, at the same time obliquely identifying Fanny as a sister figure rather than a possible lover: 'Grandpapa did right, therefore, to watch me. And yet . . . how vainly would he have watched me had I meditated any evil whispers to Fanny!'[101] Further significance is placed on the grandfather by comparing him to that pregnant De Quinceyan symbol, the crocodile, the bizarre imagery serving to turn the language into the more exotic overtones of the *Opium Confessions* and the *Suspiria*, to darken the context, and to emphasize the sense of loss:

Ah, reader! when I look back upon those days, it seems to me that all things change—all things perish. . . . If, therefore, the crocodile does *not* change, all things else undeniably *do*; even the shadow of the pyramids grows less. . . . Out of the darkness, if I happen to call back the image of Fanny, up rises suddenly from a gulf of forty years a rose in June; or, if I think for an instant of the roses in June, up rises the heavenly face of Fanny. One after the other, like

[98] Ibid. 283–4.   [99] Ibid. 285.   [100] Ibid.   [101] Ibid. 286.

the antiphonies in the choral service, rise Fanny and the rose in June, then back again the rose in June and Fanny. Then come both together, as in a chorus—roses and Fannies, Fannies and Roses, without end, thick as blossoms in paradise.[102]

The mail-coach has here progressed, in diction, cadence, and meaning, far from the comfortable humdrum of its beginnings, and it plunges into the emblazonings of De Quincey's dream language:

once again the roses call up the sweet countenance of Fanny; and she, being the granddaughter of a crocodile, awakens a dreadful host of semi-legendary animals—griffins, dragons, basilisks, sphinxes—till at length the whole vision of fighting images crowds into one towering armorial shield, a vast emblazonry of human charities and human loveliness that have perished, but quartered heraldically with unutterable and demoniac natures, whilst over all rises, as a surmounting crest, one fair female hand, with the forefinger pointing, in sweet, sorrowful admonition, upwards to heaven, where is sculptured the eternal writing which proclaims the frailty of earth and her children.[103]

When the coach is reascended, there is now the eternal agency of the feminine added to its journey; not Fanny herself, but the dimension opened up by her evocation. The coach reasserts, more strongly than ever, its social centrality and power and velocity:

What stir! what sea-like ferment!—what a thundering of wheels!—what a trampling of hoofs!—what a sounding of trumpets!—what farewell cheers—what redoubling peals of brotherly congratulation. . . . Liberated from the embarrassments of the city, and issuing into the broad uncrowded avenues of the northern suburbs, we soon begin to enter upon our natural pace of ten miles an hour.[104]

The specification of velocity, 'ten miles an hour', is the portent of an ascending scale of onrush. Talking much of women now, De Quincey focuses on one, the comfortable images of common day now long behind the coach:

. . . we changed horses an hour or two after midnight. . . . I alighted; and immediately from a dismantled stall in the street, where no doubt she had been presiding through the earlier part of the night, advanced eagerly a middle-aged woman. The sight of my newspaper it was that had drawn her attention upon myself. The victory which we were carrying down to the provinces on *this* occasion was the imperfect one of Talavera. . . . I could not but ask her if she had not some relative in the Peninsular army. Oh, yes; her only son was there. In what regiment? He was a trooper in the 23d Dragoons. My heart sank within me as she made that answer.[105]

[102] Ibid. 287, 289.   [103] Ibid. 289.   [104] Ibid. 294–5.   [105] Ibid. 298–9.

The reason De Quincey's heart sank was that the Twenty-third Dragoons had made a heroic charge that cost them dearly: 'And this, then, was the regiment . . . in which the young trooper served whose mother was now talking in a spirit of such joyous enthusiasm. Did I tell her the truth? Has I the heart to break up her dreams? No.'[106]

What he does rather is move to the next section, which is loweringly called 'The Vision of Sudden Death'. It begins with brooding reflections, and then takes up again the image of the journey of the mail-coach, which now illustrates a text for what De Quincey calls 'this reverie upon *Sudden Death*'.[107] Daylight and social conviviality have now irrevocably given way to 'the dead of night' and to De Quincey 'as a solitary spectator'.[108] The narrative is as deep-dyed in gloom as the imagination of Poe:

> . . . the mail recommenced its journey northwards about midnight. Wearied with the long detention at a gloomy hotel, I walked out about eleven o'clock at night for the sake of fresh air . . .[109]

He gets lost, however, and almost misses the coach. Midnight, misadventure, gloom, and solitude are joined by other images of the depths: 'Having mounted the box, I took a small quantity of laudanum'; this drew upon him the special attention of the coachman, and 'it drew my own attention to the fact that this coachman was a monster in point of bulk, and that he had but one eye.'[110] To compound matters, the coachman begins to drift off to sleep:

> During the first stage, I found out that Cyclops was mortal: he was liable to the shocking affection of sleep. . . . Throughout the second stage he grew more and more drowsy. In the second mile of the third stage he surrendered himself finally and without a struggle to his perilous temptation.[111]

The guard too went to sleep, and so De Quincey now drives through the night alone, the situation at once dreaded and inevitable both in the narrative and in the course of his life. The onrushing velocity has increased, too, as apocalypse nears:

> And thus at last, about ten miles from Preston, it came about that I found myself left in charge of his Majesty's London and Glasgow mail, then running at the least twelve miles an hour.[112]

Unlike the coach, the prose winds slowly along; but the sense of foreboding builds and the coach's velocity increases:

---

[106] Ibid. 299.   [107] Ibid. 304.   [108] Ibid.   [109] Ibid. 305.
[110] Ibid. 306.   [111] Ibid. 308, 309.   [112] Ibid. 309.

Suddenly . . . I was awakened to a sullen sound, as of some motion on the distant road. It stole upon the air for a moment; I listened in awe; but then it died away. Once roused, however, I could not but observe with alarm the quickened motion of our horses. Ten years' experience had made my eye learned in the valuing of motion; and I saw that we were now running thirteen miles an hour.[113]

The thirteen miles an hour has the psychological velocity almost of a space-warp. To add to the gathering sense of the ominous and ultimate, De Quincey notes that the coach is now on the wrong side of the road. The apocalyptic moment comes closer:

Under this steady though rapid anticipation of the evil which *might* be gathering ahead, ah! what a sullen mystery of fear, what a sigh of woe, was that which stole upon the air, as again the far-off sound of a wheel was heard! A whisper it was—a whisper from, perhaps, four miles off—secretly announcing a ruin that, being unforeseen, was not the less inevitable. . . . What could be done—who was it that could do it—to check the storm flight of these maniacal horses?[114]

Sweeping around an angle of the road, De Quincey perceives the scene of apocalypse:

Before us lay an avenue straight as an arrow, six hundred yards, perhaps, in length; and the umbrageous trees, which rose in a regular line from either side, meeting high overhead, gave to it the character of a cathedral aisle.[115]

The invocation of 'cathedral aisle' heightens the sense of an apocalyptic ultimate; at the end of the aisle, De Quincey, like Novalis's apprentice at Sais, sees—himself! Or rather, he sees a symbolic recapitulation of his night journey and the threatened feminine: 'a frail reedy gig, in which were seated a young man, and by his side a young lady.'[116] Never mind that the frail reedy gig, a metonymy for the threatened feminine, has just been said to have been heard from 4 miles off, as the 'far-off sound of a wheel'; that was necessary then, but now, equally necessary and entirely fitting, 'The little carriage is creeping on at one mile an hour.'[117]

Disaster seems inevitable: 'A second time I shouted'.[118] As the 'storm flight of these maniacal horses' careers towards the 'frail reedy gig', catastrophe looms for the symbolic figures; the abyss opens up; the bottomless pit yawns. But then, narrowly, breathtakingly, incredibly, ruin is averted. The young man, in a recapitulation of De Quincey's own taking-charge of his existence, reveals himself as equal to the threat:

---

[113] Ibid. 311.   [114] Ibid. 312–13.   [115] Ibid. 313–14.   [116] Ibid. 314.
[117] Ibid.   [118] Ibid.

craven he was not: sudden had been the call upon him, and sudden was his answer to the call. He saw, he heard, he comprehended the ruin that was coming down. . . . Then suddenly he rose; stood upright; and, by a powerful strain upon the reins, raising his horse's fore-feet from the ground, he slewed him round on the pivot of his hind legs, so as to plant the little equipage in a position nearly at right angles to ours. . . . faithful was he that drove to his terrific duty; faithful was the horse to *his* command. But the lady—oh! heavens! will that spectacle ever depart from my dreams, as she rose and sank upon her seat, sank and rose, threw up her arms widely to heaven. . . . In the twinkling of an eye, our flying horses had carried us to the termination of the umbrageous aisle; at right angles we wheeled into our former direction; the turn of the road carried the scene out of my eyes in an instant and swept it into my dreams forever.[119]

The twinkling of an eye that saved the symbolic figures resonates in harmony with that moment, in the twinkling of an eye, at the last trumpet, when we too shall be saved.

There follows then, legitimized by De Quincey's last statement, which links dreams and biblical prophecy, a concluding section called 'Dream Fugue: Founded on the Preceding Theme of Sudden Death'. Here, in the very language of the book of Apocalypse, De Quincey talks of his great themes, of summer, of death, of a female child, and of a trumpeter, transfigured from the trumpeter on the coach to the trumpeter at the Day of Judgement itself. 'Thou also, Dying Trumpeter, with thy love that was victorious, and thy anguish that was finishing, didst enter the tumult; trumpet and echo—farewell love, and farewell anguish—rang through the dreadful *sanctus*.'[120] At the end of the fugue and of the essay, De Quincey sounds his deepest and most characteristic note, the death and hoped-for restoration of his sister.

The Easter dream about the resurrection of the prostitute Ann had been characterized by the sweetness of the personal. In taking up the Book of Revelation's words, 'And God shall wipe away all tears from their eyes; and there shall be no more death, nor sorrow, nor crying, neither shall there be any more pain',[121] Ann's resurrection is filled with the tenderness of personal reunion:

Seventeen years ago, when the lamp-light fell upon her face, as for the last time I kissed her lips (lips, Ann, that to me were not polluted!), her eyes were streaming with tears; the tears were now wiped away; she seemed more beautiful than she was at that time, but in all other points the same, and not older.[122]

---

[119] Ibid. 315–18.   [120] Ibid. 326.   [121] Rev. 21: 4.
[122] De Quincey, *Confessions*, 98.

The tears that were wiped away from the eyes of Ann are those same tears that Milton, affected also by the promise of the Book of Revelation, had wiped from the eyes of Lycidas. For the saints, who entertain Lycidas in heaven, and sing, and singing in their glory move, will 'wipe the tears for ever from his eyes.'[123]

The resurrection at the end of 'The English Mail Coach' is informed too by the Book of Revelation. But it is different in tone and focus. Resurrection now has about it the thunder and trumpets of apocalypse, not the tenderness of the personal, and it now places the restored image of the sister, not in the matrix of sweetness, but in the matrix of power and triumphant finality:

> Lo! As I looked back for seventy leagues through the mighty cathedral, I saw the quick and the dead that sang together to God, together that sang to the generations of man. All the hosts of jubilation, like armies that ride in pursuit, moved with one step. . . . [S]uddenly did God relent, suffered thy angel to turn aside His arm, and even in thee, sister unknown! shown to me for a moment only to be hidden forever, found an occasion to glorify His goodness. A thousand times, amongst the phantoms of sleep, have I seen thee entering the gates of the golden dawn, with the secret word riding before thee, with the armies of the grave behind thee—. . . a thousand times in the world of sleep have seen thee followed by God's angel through storms, . . . through dreams and the dreadful revelations that are in dreams; only that at the last, with one sling of His victorious arm, He might snatch thee back from ruin and might emblazon in thy deliverance the endless resurrection of His love:[124]

With this paean to 'the endless resurrection of His love', 'The English Mail Coach' reaches simultaneously its climax and its conclusion, a conclusion that emphasizes the endless resurrection of De Quincey's own love for his sister even as it celebrates the endless resurrection of divine love. One of the final guarantees of the Book of Revelation is that in the New Jerusalem 'there shall be no night'.[125] As the English mail-coach wheels into the courtyard of apocalypse, its journey to the end of night breaks and ceases in the abrogation of night. So totally unanticipated amid the jovial and commonplace detail of the essay's beginning, as amid the lowering gloom of its later sections, such a conclusion of apocalypse, we realize, is suddenly both fitting and inevitable. (Indeed, the spirit of the age broods over the invocations of

---

123 Milton, *Lycidas*, l. 181.   124 *De Quincey*, xiii. 326–7.
125 Rev. 22: 5.

apocalypse with which 'The English Mail Coach' concludes,[126] as can be shown, to adduce a single example, by the writings of M. H. Abrams[127]). The apocalyptic finale is exactly appropriate for the mail-coach's journey to the end of night, and for the parallel journey that constituted the man De Quincey's life. And it is, as well, the final recapitulation that annuls and cancels further need of recapitulation. So much for apocalypse. So much too for De Quincey's recapitulations. In a larger matrix, the lives and works of all three of the great essayists recapitulate fundamental features of the Romantic experience. De Quincey, Hazlitt, Lamb; Lamb, Hazlitt, De Quincey: all are connected peaks in the great range of Romanticism.

The Romantic upheaval cast up the terrain of the modern world, even as it engendered the collapse of age-old fortifications for the spirit. Among those who struggled and strove amid the debris of the epoch, and who managed significant achievement despite disorientation and perplexity, three who were honoured in their own day of Romantic turmoil, and who will continue to be honoured in the retrospections of future eras, which will have their own travails of the spirit, were Charles Lamb, William Hazlitt, and Thomas De Quincey. To retrace their paths will always be to ascend into the great Romantic range, with the elevation and boulder-strewn slope of Samuel Taylor Coleridge in line of sight ahead.

[126] In a lecture delivered at the Wordsworth Summer Conference at Dove Cottage on 5 Aug. 1985, entitled 'Pursuing the Throne of God: De Quincey's Prose and the Evangelical Revival', Grevel Lindop referred the pervasive use of apocalyptic language and imagery in De Quincey's writings to his mother's involvement with the Claphamite revival of millenarian Christianity (the lecture was subsequently published in *The Charles Lamb Bulletin*, New Series 7, no. 52 (1986), 97–111). Cf. De Quincey: 'My mother's views were precisely those of her friend Mrs Hannah More, of Wilberforce, of Henry Thornton, of Zachary Macaulay (father of the historian), and generally of those who were then known amongst sneerers as "the Clapham saints"' (*De Quincey*, i. 407).

[127] See M. H. Abrams, 'Apocalypse: Theme and Romantic Variations', *The Correspondent Breeze: Essays on English Romanticism* (New York: W. W. Norton & Company, 1984), 225–57; M. H. Abrams, *Natural Supernaturalism: Tradition and Revolution in Romantic Literature* (New York: W. W. Norton & Company, Inc., 1971), 37–65, 329–56.

Index

128

INDEX

Sandford, Mrs Henry 108 n.
Sand, George 5
Schelling, Friedrich Wilhelm Joseph
  von 77, 111
Schiller, Johann Christoph Friedrich
  49, 79
Schlegel, August Wilhelm 4, 12
Schlegel, Friedrich 1, 4, 5, 6, 11, 12, 23,
  37, 53
Schmidt, Erich 31 n.
Schneider, Elisabeth 90
Schoenbaum, Samuel 106 n.
Schopenhauer, Arthur 4
Scott, Sir Walter 4, 16, 17
Senancour, Étienne de 5, 8, 9, 22, 99
Shakespeare, William 4 n., 42 n., 56
Shawcross, John 12 n.
Shelley, Mary 7
Shelley, Percy Bysshe 1, 7, 9, 12, 16, 18,
  19, 23, 25, 37, 38, 53, 60;
  'Marianne's Dream' 60; 'Mont Blanc'
  7, 9; 'The Triumph of Life' 60; 'The
  Witch of Atlas' 60
Shklar, Judith 30
Simmons, Ann 35
Socinus, Faustus 77
solitude 5, 6 n., 13, 19, 56 n., 91 n., 98,
  118; as criterion of Romanticism 5,
  6 n., 13, 19, 99
Sophocles 76
South, Robert 76
Southey, Robert 2, 18, 25, 37, 39 n., 78,
  81 n., 82, 105; his anger at De
  Quincey 105 n.
Spenser, Edmund 4
Spinoza, Benedict de 7, 77
spirit of the age 1, 8, 14, 121
Stevenson, Robert Louis 57
Strauss, David Friedrich 7
streams 9, 10, 11; see also currents; rivers
Strich, Fritz 10
sublimity (sublime) 3, 4 n., 7, 11, 72
suicide 6 n., 13, 20, 30, 31
Swabey, William Curtis 6 n.
Swedenborg, Emanuel 77
Swift, Jonathan 77, 112
symbol 10, 13, 19, 98, 116

Talfourd, Thomas N. 65 n., 66 n.
Taylor, Jeremy 77
Thierry, J.-J. 29 n.
Thomson, James 77
Thornton, Henry 122 n.
Tillotson, Geoffrey 25
Tillotson, John 77
Tilly, Alexandre, comte de 29
torrents 7, 8, 9, 18; see also currents;
  rivers; streams
Trelawny, Edward John 12 n., 23

Uhland, Johann Ludwig 10 n., 37

Vauban, Sébastien le Prestre de 46
Vigny, Alfred Victor, comte de 6
Volta, Alessandro, count 7
Voltaire (François Marie Arouet) 77

Walker, Sarah 53, 86
wanderlust 23, 37, 96
Wasserman, Earl 27
Watson, Seth B. 8 n.
Wedgwood, Thomas 83, 84
Wellek, René 13, 112
White, R. J. 12 n.
Wilberforce, William 122 n.
Wollstonecraft, Mary 84
Woodhouse, Richard, friend of Keats
  93
Wordsworth, Catharine 102, 103, 106
Wordsworth, Dorothy 93 n., 106 n., 107
Wordsworth, William 1, 7, 9, 10 n., 15,
  18, 23, 25, 31 n., 33, 34, 36, 37, 38,
  39 n., 44 n., 51, 53, 69, 84, 99, 105,
  107, 111; his anger at De Quincey
  106; his arrogance 107-8; his
  disapproval of Hazlitt 81-2, 85 n.; his
  Immortality Ode 28-9; his originality
  60; his praise of Lamb 51-2; his
  relationship to De Quincey 106-8;
  his reticence about his personal life
  106

Young, G. M. 61

Zisca, John 77